Praise for Marina Vishmidt

'Marina's intellectual practice truly constituted a form of praxis, and her work was always situated in a commonly sensed world. Thinking with Marina by reading her, following her through so many encounters with other practices, is to feel the tender exhilaration of negation. She was never interested in branding herself through quasi-proprietary concepts. While Marina did, of course, develop crucial concepts such as infrastructural critique, those need to be seen as part of a method that operationalises rather than fetishizes them. Guy Debord (who was not necessarily Marina's favourite) once noted that, according to the dominant standards, the style of dialectical theory is a scandal because, "while it makes concrete use of existing concepts, it simultaneously recognizes their rediscovered fluidity and their inevitable destruction." In those terms, Marina's work is wonderfully scandalous'

Sven Lütticken, author of *Objections*

'Marina's blazingly brilliant theories about infrastructure and labour help light the path for every student, critic, artist, and activist who is engaged in collective struggle towards a more just art world'

Julia Bryan-Wilson, professor of contemporary art and LGBTQ+ studies, Columbia University

'Marina Vishmidt's final text is a brilliant study of what art remains bound to and what it is bound for. Negation is the motor of possibility, and it might not be too late to erase our own alibis. There is no world but the world'

Anne Boyer, author of *Garments Against Women*

'What is to be undone? How? With whom? Ensnared in capital's negative totality, it is tempting to imagine that we can find refuge in experiences of care, reproduction, and life before and beyond capitalism or, alternatively, that we can decree capital's integral abolition. In this indispensable book, Marina Vishmidt – with the intransigent generosity that marked her life and work – demonstrates that "critique as a material practice of antagonism" must eschew abstract radicalism to fight instead on the terrain of infrastructure, where value and waste, relations of production and relations of destruction, intersect. Vishmidt teaches us that "there is no opposition between breaking and building." *Infrastructural Critique* is an irreplaceable invitation and guide to the work of abolition'

Alberto Toscano, author of *Late Fascism*

'Marina Vishmidt's rigorous examination of the many facets of reproduction is essential for understanding the systems of relations guaranteeing capital's accumulation and its potential subversion. This insightful book will be valuable to theorists and organizers alike invested in subverting the reproduction of value and in building a different world held in common'

Silvia Federici, author of *Caliban and the Witch*

'Vishmidt speaks with unfailing clarity about how value feeds on devastation and how art's institutions sit inside the chain of extraction rather than outside or above. *Infrastructural Critique* is essential reading for anyone who despite all is not ready to give up on the artworld as a place for collective struggle. What makes this book, her last gift to us, so generative is that it never stops at the diagnosis: between reproduction and abolition it opens ground for new forms'

Anselm Franke, curator and author

'Vishmidt's articulate and incisive volume examines the conditions under which art is made and circulated. Here, solidarity is not an ideal, but a necessary strategy capable of antagonising and retooling the infrastructures that organise everyday life and culture. An essential handbook for cultural workers seeking to understand and transform their workplace, this is nothing short of a call for a collective rebellion'

Mason Leaver-Yap, cultural worker

Marina's friendship and the fruits of her incredible mind have been 'an irreplaceable source of nourishment for the part of ourselves that is the weakest, the sickest, the least equipped to resist the harshness of the present circumstances, precisely because it is the part that will carry us when this present is abolished and new forms of freedom and intelligence revive the dying world. *Infrastructural Critique* looks systematically into all the unsolvable issues of our failed struggles, our poverty, our entrapments and our incapacity to fight back against the forces that are not just undermining our political position, but threatening the possibility of life on Earth. And yet it leaves us the tools to navigate all this with an accrued sense of reality, one that brings us back to this Earth that is ours where she no longer walks with us. Pragmatic and anti-moral, in her distinctively visionary way, Marina's writings are both an unreachable horizon of sharpness and a safe place where everything makes sense for us'

Claire Fontaine, artist and author of *Human Strike*

Marina Vishmidt (1976–2024) was a philosopher, organiser and art theorist. A lecturer at Goldsmiths, University of London and professor of art theory at the University of Applied Arts Vienna, she was one of the major critical theorists of her generation. Her writing spanned art theory, feminist social reproduction theory, finance, ecology, labour and labour organising, value-form theory, Black studies and film. Her first book was *Speculation as a Mode of Production: Forms of Value-Subjectivity in Art and Capital* (2018).

Infrastructural Critique

Contemporary Art between Reproduction and Abolition

Marina Vishmidt

Edited by Larne Abse Gogarty, Danny Hayward, Kerstin Stakemeier

VERSO
London • New York

First published by Verso 2026

The manufacturer's authorised representative in the EU for product safety (GPSR) is LOGOS EUROPE, 9 rue Nicolas Poussin, 17000, La Rochelle, France
contact@logoseurope.eu

1 3 5 7 9 10 8 6 4 2

Verso
UK: 6 Meard Street, London W1F 0EG
US: 207 32nd Street, New York, NY 10016
versobooks.com

Verso is the imprint of New Left Books

ISBN-13: 978-1-83674-159-6
ISBN-13: 978-1-83674-161-9 (US EBK)
ISBN-13: 978-1-83674-160-2 (UK EBK)

British Library Cataloguing in Publication Data
A catalogue record for this book is available from the British Library

Library of Congress Cataloging-in-Publication Data

Names: Vishmidt, Marina, 1976– author | Gogarty, Larne Abse editor | Hayward, Danny editor | Stakemeier, Kerstin, 1975– editor
Title: Infrastructural critique : contemporary art between reproduction and abolition / Marina Vishmidt ; edited by Larne Abse Gogarty, Danny Hayward, Kerstin Stakemeier.
Description: London ; New York : Verso, 2026. | Includes bibliographical references and index.
Identifiers: LCCN 2026028873 (print) | LCCN 2026028874 (ebook) | ISBN 9781836741596 paperback | ISBN 9781836741619 ebk
Subjects: LCSH: Art museums
Classification: LCC N430 .V57 2026 (print) | LCC N430 (ebook)
LC record available at https://lccn.loc.gov/2026028873
LC ebook record available at https://lccn.loc.gov/2026028874

Typeset in Sabon LT by Hewer Text UK Ltd, Edinburgh
Printed and bound by CPI Group (UK) Ltd, Croydon, CR0 4YY

Contents

Preface by Stefano Harney and Fred Moten ix

Introduction: A Life Lived in Different Circumstances by Danny Hayward 1

PART I. FOUNDATIONS

1. Speculative Infrastructures 37
2. Critique, Institutional and Infrastructural 65
3. Infrastructure, Interrupted 89

PART II. CRYSTAL DRILLS

4. Reproduction 113
5. Entropy 137
6. Abolition 155

Conclusion: Critique Is the Cutting Tool, Not the Price of Admission 179

Acknowledgements 185
Index 189

Preface

What Love's Got to Do with It

It is impossible to hold on to art today, but somehow, we can't let go. It is not that the evidence is hidden from us. We know exactly where art is housed, valued and sold; and it is nowhere anyone should want to be; and there we are, looking for beauty.

As for artists today, they are not just figures drawn into capitalism or into subject formation. They are the archetype. We don't need an aesthetic education anymore (and we don't get one) in the universities. We are artists. The production line of subjects has been discarded as too costly and too prone to defects. It is easier and safer to reverse-engineer directly from the artist into the worker-as-entrepreneur, whom Marx describes. To work without end, without pay, and without any distinction between work and life, and with an almost psychotic commitment to innovate and market those innovations. Sounds familiar.

And the artwork is now largely incidental, not just to this new process, but to capital itself. With the securitisation of the art world, the artwork has become speculative, a derivative of something else, not quite the artist's labour. This labour itself has become labour in general, abstracted in the first instance through collective effort – gallerists, critics, directors, academics, fabricators – but, beyond this work in common, abstracted by securitisation, that is by the full integration of the artworld into finance. Finance has overcome the fungibility problem of the artwork by substituting it for the artist in general, a scarcity that keeps popping up like a bad penny. And when the speculative bubble bursts, there is nothing an individual artist can make, or a pleading academic could say, to change the price direction. All that can be said is that it's a good time to buy. Still, it seems we have to live with art to preserve beauty just as it seems we have to act politically in order to practise the sociality that surrounds politics. But our condition is chronic. Art and politics incarcerate that by which they are released. We are held in this unnatural nest of boxes, this concentric circling of enclosures, this counter-subsistent order and its terms, this repression of mess and suppression of mass in omnicidal regulation. We've been framed, and it's breaking our heart.

With the facts staring us in the face, why don't we walk away? This is the question Marina Vishmidt begins to answer in her brilliant book. Against the speculation of capital, she deploys her speculative negativity. She finds a thread of artists stretching from Mierle Laderman Ukeles to Cameron Rowland who are ready and able to address the abstract labour and property relations not just at the heart of the artworld but at the heart of racial capitalism and its consigliere, Kantian common sense. Drawing on Negt and Kluge, illuminating them, scribbling in their margins, she discovers through these artists that the society of producers never gives up its desires so fully as to reach objectivity, and therefore never loses its capacity to resist.

Marina's constant emphasis on construction, on making as the mode of speculative negation, cuts against the grain of the abstract, positive, positional speculation that dominates the art world and that presents itself for smooth assimilation into finance capital. This comes through in practice, in her careful, attentive observance of art works and performances, which she sees through to the fecundity into which they fade and in which they're felt against the cultivated, barren grain of individual appearance. She insists upon seeing the glittering infrastructure of the art world not just as material for repurposing, not just for a work-around, but in terms of its paucity, its failure of imagination, and most important its vulnerability to complete overhaul.

Key to the optimism of Marina's negative speculation is her engagement with Black studies. Here she finds not just the two-pronged attack she needs on capital and race but evidence of things not seen with and through, and of an inseparability of faith among the fated – Robinson's ontological totality. She tells us she seeks to move from institution to infrastructure and from critique to antagonism. Here she finds antagonism in its highest and deepest forms, and ready to go further. In her hands she constructs this antagonism as speculative so as not to abstract it from the struggles it animates but to permit this antagonism to ask its question: what are we doing? What are we undoing? Or in the words of George Jackson 'my enemies are institutions and any men with vested interests in them, even if that interest is only a wage'. And if it turns out that we ourselves are our own worst enemies, then what are we doing if we are not undoing our selves?

If selflessness can be emphatic, all but exemplary, so that it might be sampled, then Marina is our guide. She turns to the senses and the social, where there's a riot and a party going on. And this turn, which returns to beauty, which is negative, which fucks everything up with love, demands a turn through, if not quite against, art. Marina loves, and fights for, beauty. It is that love in which she turns and returns. This is why she turns to art the way she does. This is why she turns on art the way she does. This is why she returns to art the way she does. This is why she turns through art the way she does.

Marina shows us that the aesthete's concern was always tasteful, always moral, always somehow both interior and universal, so that even the immoral, even unto what is perceived as profligate, confirms and substantiates sovereign judgement. She shares the insight that art is all about this false convergence of morality and autonomy; that it images what sets the terms of that morality; and that beauty really has nothing to do with that. She says the sociality of the sensory, and the sensuality of the social, where beauty resides in the aesthesis we share and hear and shift and soothe and savour, work against the theory of art and the theory of mind in the leisurely existence of necessarily racial, necessarily sexual capital. She serves the aesthetic experience we share, which is messy and residual, which is always running all over and all out of itself, which cannot stand alone, which is a general strike, or an infrastructural spring.

Beauty infuses art but it refuses framing. It confuses autonomy. It's good, and it tastes like something that sounds like something. It seems like nothing, or it knows not seems. It seems like nothing's or not knowing's where it's coming from. It tastes like something but it's not in good taste but it's true. It strains against and undermines and overcomes the lies that tell of it, which are not of but are rather arrayed against appearance. It's real like that. It's like Marina, looking with us, in our eyes. As a matter of fact, at the corner of Rosa Luxemburg and Exene Cervenka, it *is* Marina, for beauty, with love.

Stefano Harney and Fred Moten

Introduction

A Life Lived in Different Circumstances

1.

Maybe it starts with hopping turnstiles in the NYC subway en route to the movies. The Angelika at the Cable Building in Manhattan's Greenwich Village, 'the most successful arthouse in the United States'; the late 1990s; the history of NYC fare evasion. Minor negation, in a major key. A relationship of art to infrastructure begins somewhere ordinary like this, in the basic everyday, with material conditions and the desire for culture as the two postulates of a life's dialectical opening sequence.

'This last . . . loops back to the first,' Marina once wrote to me,

> having had no opportunity to travel out of New York State for the first 20 years of my life, there's still an indecent patina of class mobility in travelling a lot, a constant flaunting of the un-necessity of everything I can do or be.

Marina Vishmidt was born in 1976 in Kharkiv and made her way to New York with her mother and grandparents when she was three, joining the exodus from the Soviet Union to the United States (the so-called dropouts) after Jewish emigration was permitted in the 1970s. She studied at the Bronx High School of Science, made zines, read all the fiction in the local library and went to Sarah Lawrence College, around an hour upstate. She 'always seemed to know', wrote her friend Dimitra Kotouza, 'where she wanted to be and how to get there by mobilising the scarcest of resources'.[1] The image of her mobilising scarce resources by skipping fare gates comes from memories of friends during her undergraduate years, but perhaps it feels like something 'from the movies' as well; so reality and representation have already arrived at a point of indifference, or indeterminacy: the same point that the teenager who skipped turnstiles would later invoke when she wrote a book titled *Speculation as a Mode of Production*, a work in which aesthetic representation and economic 'infrastructure' constantly pass over and into one another, operate on one another, becoming indeterminate, at a level of abstraction that can feel painful, splendid, transformative and bewildering.

So it starts with hopping turnstiles in the NYC subway en route to the movies, with the tiniest conceivable little nick in the total system of value relations, really something barely even perceptible, and then it widens. In her theoretical work, Marina came to think early on of conceptual abstraction as the scarcest or scantiest resource of them all, a shadow that dances across some things, a thing not a thing in itself, desperately close to being nothing, a negation, a mere 'hole in what it is not'.[2] Later, she would argue that what she called conceptual 'indeterminacy' is one simple result of abstract identification, of the type art is (equal to) capital, or speculation is (equal to) a mode of production. It opens up a little nick, a cut, in which neither term is the necessary one – a gap through which you can glimpse an entire worldview.[3]

Marina moved to London in 1998, aged twenty-one. She skipped the turnstile of the UK border system by means of a fake

1 Mute Collective, 'The Conditions of Possibility: Tributes to Marina Vishmidt 1976–2024' (2024), metamute.org.

2 'A thing is a whole in a thing it is not': Marina was a fan of this koan by a conceptual artist who need not be named.

3 For one important source of this idea, see Paolo Virno, *The Grammar of the Multitude*, translated by Isabello Bertoletti et al., New York: Semiotext(e), 2004, 77.

marriage, worked at the artists' moving image organisation LUX, made a number of experimental Super 8 films, and fell in with the writers, filmmakers and musicians around the politics and culture magazine *Mute*. She studied philosophy at Middlesex, wrote her thesis on Andrei Tarkovsky's *Solaris* and Gilles Deleuze; published essays on bears, cartography, precarity, jetpacks and gentrification; refined her taste in macabre, absurdist children's literature; and worked a lot, initially in the early 2000s London service economy – bar jobs, food catering jobs, film extra jobs, nighttime press clippings jobs. In the now unthinkable landscape of Blairite law and order, squats and dying open-source activism, the terrain of her aesthetic tastes was characterised by fantastical machines, recursive topography and the 'elaborate, grotesque and impenetrable lyrical apparatus' of Mark E. Smith of The Fall; and the terrain of her political ones by Italian *autonomia* and the US collective Midnight Notes. Later, as she 'got into the world of living off my brain', she began to apply the writings of Marx and Adorno to post-1960s conceptual art, a line of inquiry that would culminate, some years later, in her PhD, and eventually in her first solo-authored book, *Speculation as a Mode of Production: Forms of Value-Subjectivity in Art and Capital*. She screened anti-work films in squats, wrote essays on education struggles, travelled a lot, and participated, when time permitted, in a years-long series of discussions about the financial crisis led by London communists and anarchists in the upstairs rooms of East London pubs, in one of which, one Friday night in late January 2011, I met her for the first time.

The discussion that night was about 'communisation theory'. I arrived late to a small meeting room already full, crammed with the people who would become the major figures in my life. 'Communisation', the theory group *Endnotes* had written, in the first issue of their journal two years earlier, 'is the immediate production of communism: the self-abolition of the proletariat through its abolition of capital and state.'[4] For several years, that thesis would simply be there, in the air of post-financial crisis social movements, a kind of shibboleth. The word itself had the properties of a magical formula, and so even when it was used as an in-joke, an ironic wish fulfilment fantasy, or as a byword for long 'lists of things to be abolished', it was inescapable.[5] Later, the person who I remember that night speaking in long branching sentences and gazing intently at her split ends while she was listening would write at length about *Endnotes*' analysis, in particular in relation to 'surplus populations', logistics, gender and race; though it was the second part of the thesis quoted earlier, the 'self-abolition ... through ... abolition of capital and state', that most attracted her attention, giving direction to an inquiry that she would carry out with many collaborators across many settings and which culminates – prematurely – in her concept of 'infrastructural critique'. Years later, she would write to me that the idea of the subject skipping over the turnstile of itself could not help 'but evoke ... the image of Baron Munchausen pulling himself out of the hole by his own hair, or the Russian idiom "you can't leap over yourself"'.[6] As a theorist of (self-)abolition, she always wanted to find ways to deepen the paradox, to elude the carnival strongman game of 'radical politics' as a futile test of virility. But what she appreciated in the schema was the challenge to think the transformation of subject and objective conditions *together*, in the same breath, for which task the programme of

4 'Afterword', *Endnotes* 1 (2008), endnotes.org.

5 P. Valentine, 'The Gender Rift in Communisation' (2012), metamute.org.

6 Marina Vishmidt and Danny Hayward, 'Self-dissolution to the left of me, self-dissolution to the right: A political glossary of self-overcomings' (2018), 7, vishmidt.memoryoftheworld.org.

infrastructural critique supplies the statement of an experimental artistic and political method.

Via the history of taste, it is possible to write a sort of shadow biography, an account of a life that never wanted to account for itself, 'Points on a libidinal map'.[7] Marina preferred low modernism to high, Witold Gombrowicz to James Joyce, situational comedy to polemical denunciation, Félix Guattari to Guy Debord. She preferred Viktor Shklovsky to Vladimir Mayakovsky, Lisa Crystal Carver to Kathleen Hanna, Shulamith Firestone to Valerie Solanas, De La Soul to Public Enemy. She liked the late Marx more than the young, and the eccentric and carnivalesque films of Ulrike Ottinger more than the semiotically precise and theoretically overdetermined ones of Laura Mulvey. She enjoyed reflexive negation, Edward Gorey, Herk Harvey's *Carnival of Souls* and Cameron Rowland's infrastructural critique more than the grandstanding floridities of the transgressive avant-garde, and she prized the eccentric, ironic and grotesque, the fabulous machines of Raymond Roussel's *Locus Solus*, over everything rhetorically declamatory, consummate and self-affirming. She disliked improvised public speaking and preferred to carry out her operations from an askew or alternative stage, ignoring the principled objections that ring out in tiny self-asserting voices from the limelight. In 2007, she wrote a text titled 'The Humorous Dimension of Time', in which a familiar character appears in the style of an avatar:

> A radiant young engineer busies himself, to the delight of onlookers, in arranging and rearranging Lilliputian modules of the City of the Soviets on a small platform extending from a proscenium arch. Toy cranes dispose the buildings

7 Marina Vishmidt and Lisa Jay Jeschke, 'Work Breaks Us, We Break Work', in *365 Days of Invisible Work*, Leipzig: Spector Books, 2017.

> here and there. From inside some of them, principled objections ring out in tiny voices: 'Help! Moscow, where are you going?' – 'God save us!' – 'They're moving houses like furniture these days!'[8]

Marina would never want to be defined in relation to her origins – that was the whole point – but it is impossible to talk about her without her objects, the objects of desire through which she defined her negativity, a reflexive abstraction at the level of the subject and an endless landscape of the imperfect, ludic and changeable at the level of its materials. It begins with Miss Mary Mack and zines and the Angelika at the Cable Building in Manhattan's Greenwich Village, and it ends and begins again in the book *Infrastructural Critique*, on a desiring trajectory that has nothing to do with the rectilinear and uninteresting 'progress' that characterises a typical academic life. Marina never wanted to be a teacher. She wanted, at first, to be an artist, and in her characteristically askew and singular way she always was one. She felt herself to be a 'diffident' public speaker, found asserting herself intimidating and shrank from it wilfully, in search of a 'space which was purely motoric but also impressionable', wanting 'to have as little resistance to the brutality of novelty or sociality which I knew I could not understand and there was no point throwing myself against it'. She experienced competition 'viscerally as a burning sensation, and subjectively as one of the greatest impoverishments/abjections imaginable', and she grew up as an immigrant in a single-parent family with scarce resources, immersing herself in literature, cinema and art in that order in a search for the means of movement that was never secured to her as a right. Her negativity was her style and her sense of humour

8 Marina Vishmidt, 'The Humorous Dimension of Time', in *Mobile Cinema*, edited by Romana Schmalisch, Berlin: Archive Books, 2017.

a reaction to social experience and the feeling of subjective and rhetorical impoverishment before it was anything like a philosophical 'position', which helps to explain why her theoretical preferences were in complete defiance of any conventional canon of academic coherence. To be *un-necessary*, to be nothing but that, to be nothing but the un-necessity of the state of affairs through which you are defined, conditioned and deformed; to see yourself not as the bearer of negativity but as its *object*; to identify *with* negativity as the possibility of difference or change in things, including the thing that you are, means to want to be no more than negativity because to be more than this is to be less than what it is possible to be, in an approach in which there is no firm ground on which to stand, and no standpoint other than the constant movement through and against our own conditions, in a society defined by private ownership and the relentless accumulation of capital. 'Elements of negation already make up what you are, no less than what you are capable of becoming' (*Speculation as a Mode of Production*):[9] this is the slogan of the person who defines herself neither through her material conditions, as per the logic of identitarian institutional 'class politics', nor through the hypothesis of one or another kind of abstract transcendence (humanism, mysticism) but through the movement of opposition to them, a movement of negativity that can take place on every scale running from this sentence to the turnstiles of a city's public transport system to its cultural institutions and financial architectures all the way through to the totality of material social relationships on which all of these depend, where

9 The exact quote is 'elements of negation already make up what they [social forms] are, no less than what they are capable of becoming'. Marina Vishmidt, *Speculation as a Mode of Production: Forms of Value Subjectivity in Art and Capital*, Leiden: Brill, 2018, 83. The individual is also a 'social form', of course.

contemporary, 'post-conceptual' art plays its tiny, walk-on role, and makes its incision.

2.

There are many different ways to understand the project that Marina gave the working title 'from institutional to infrastructural critique', but one way is to understand it is as being about contradiction. Its title is a contradiction, suggesting that the quintessential superstructure or 'sphere of representation', the art institution, is itself conceivable in Marxist terms as an 'infrastructure', a base. In the current presentation of that project, so is the title of the first chapter, the central thesis of the second, and the normative horizon of the third, as well as the substantive content of the dialectical philosophy on which Marina often draws, which in her thinking always exists alongside a philosophy of difference that rejects it, in contradiction to the claims to self-sufficiency of both.

In a 2017 text written for a film produced by the short-lived feminist art collective Channels, Marina offered some informal thoughts about what she considered the 'personality' of waste, contradiction or non-identity:

> I am less interested in positive appropriations of waste time. I hate care. I like the idea of 'staying with the trouble', but also see how in the current structure of society this often shades off into indulgence. I am worried about the whole concept of indulgence though as well, and the notions of abjected stuckness and inutility it reinforces, gendered notions. So perhaps it's not a good direction to take either. I am not sure about reappropriation of anything, as reappropriation feeds into a cycle of reification, though it can also

be thrown out of it. I feel uneasy about so much of radical thought's lack of interest in, or we could even say care for, contradiction, and its love for new words as if they mapped onto things, rather than loving the words for their opacity. Waste itself has a dynamic and a personality that does not need to be recuperated but expanded as an angry, loving detachment from what keeps us running in place, whether it's driven by axioms of care, or work, or profit. Taking up space in the sink, taking space.

In many ways, this short film contains the entire problem of infrastructural critique as she would go on to develop it. In the opening sequences, we see a picture of four women eating together, while another bathes naked in the sink of a women's squat in Rosetta Street, South London, in 1974, along with images of Marina's own kitchen in Hackney, East London, shot through a wall-hatch from the living room next door (see image overleaf). 'Generally,' Marina suggests gently on the voiceover, 'washing is not conversational' and 'does not usually share space with dinner parties'. Yet the 'mediations', or, more simply, the walls in this image have collapsed, and, in place of two distinct reproductive and social 'institutions', we see the sinuous outlines of one, a domestic Moebius strip: 'a home dwells folded into itself as an institution and then transits as if whole and unharmed into another institution, so a ground that also feels like a container'.

Like in so much of Marina's writing, at least from the time of her Master's thesis on Deleuze's 'The Brain Is the Screen', 'a reversible continuum is glimpsed'. Indeterminacy between distinct domains *begins* as the result of an abstract identification, the outcome of an insinuated copula between the logically diverse and notionally distinct – but it *becomes* a way of introducing a gap or inserting an opening within norms of conventional or prescribed use, similar, in its way, to the gap introduced into the

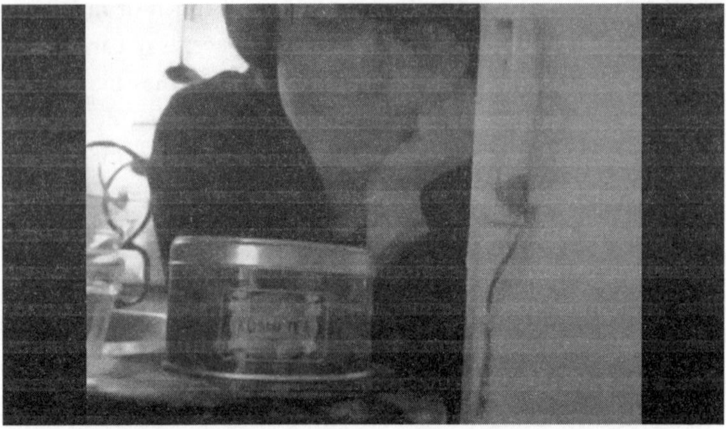

Channels, *This Is a Window*, 2017. Video still of film, by Channels (Marina Vishmidt, Rose-Anne Gush, Christina Chalmers, Larne Abse-Gogarty, Hannah Proctor, Amy Tobin, Rachel Baker and Lizzie Homersham). Image by Danny Hayward

unbroken system of value relations by teenagers jumping over a turnstile. Marina's interest in this (perhaps unusually literal) conceptual move has a few distinct philosophical sources, but the insistently materialist inflection of her treatment of it flows back to an insight most often associated with 1970s Marxist-feminism: the concept, the norm (surplus value, wage labour) is reproduced through something outside of itself (wage labour, housework), *its structural exception*; and the two terms are dynamically co-constitutive. In this case, the 'institution of the social' (the dinner party) appears in the film *as something needing to be reproduced*, demanding of resources from another institution outside of it (the institution of domestic labour); and this second institution is capable of being 'folded in' to the institution of the social itself, by means of an unexpected collapsing of differences – here of the differences conventionally distinguishing bathroom and dining room. Conceptual indeterminacy as open plan.

In the language of the film-essay quoted earlier, the 'conceptual' or 'perceptual' frames of the art institution theorised by Michael Asher in the 1970s, and reasserted by Andrea Fraser in 2005, have been displaced, bringing 'conditions into the frame'.[10] Or, rather, the frame remains the object, but only insofar as the conditions themselves become a frame. Thus the continuum reverses:

1. 'the frame' excludes the material conditions of the institution that make possible its status as a sphere of representation. Just as there is no dinner party without kitchen work, there is no art without reproductive labour;
2. yet, the material conditions in this case are themselves a frame, only now not a picture frame but the frame of a kitchen hatch in which reproductive work occurs, and not just of any kitchen but of Marina's kitchen, the kitchen of a privately rented East London ex-council flat in which she and several other collaborators on the film had lived, worked, made art, cooked and hosted dinner parties since 2003;

and so we finish where we began. The structure of the film is deliberately recursive; and recursion is in some ways Marina's primary method of approach to theoretical concepts. If, classically 'recursion' occurs in cinema when 'we see a painting on a wall in a film scene, and, later, the characters walk into the painting and it becomes the mise en scéne of the fictional universe, with the rest of the film being absorbed into it',[11] here, Marina,

---

10 Andrea Fraser, 'From the Critique of Institutions to an Institution of Critique', *Artforum*, 44, 1 (September 2005), 278–86.

11 Marina Vishmidt, 'A Short Introduction to Reproductive Realism', talk given at the launch for *Materials* special issue 'Economic Ophelia', 6 February 2015, vishmidt.memoryoftheworld.org.

the author of that sentence, is doing it herself, strolling into the 'frame' of institutional critique which has become the frame of the hatch in her own kitchen; and the strategic crumbling of conceptual mediations again supplies us with a point of indistinction: social reproduction – speculation as a mode of production – infrastructural critique.

So, Marina looks out at us, through the hatch, with her cheek resting on her left hand, a tin of tea that she liked placed unassumingly in the foreground, and a *mise en abyme* opens up, stretching backwards through the sequence of her own collective activities: making dinner for friends, making feminist art about social reproduction theory, making off-kilter theoretical texts about cult Italian horror movies in which American real estate investors get sucked into a gruesome painting on the wall, 'with the rest of the film being absorbed into it', as in *maître du macabre* Lucio Fulci's *Beyond* (1981),[12] 'each level pointing to the other one'. And, in the best tradition of Benjaminian dream allegory, her kitchen becomes his vision of hell, 'a vast grey landscape in which nothing lives', a zone of abjected stuckness, inutility and waste, of opacity and metamorphosis and speculative contradiction. 'Something forces us to think,' Marina often wrote, in fidelity to her love for the early Deleuze. And yet the movement stretches further back still, to illuminate something more basic: a thought about the uses of speculative method itself. Because if speculative identities like 'speculation as a mode of production' or 'infrastructural critique' fold into themselves differences thought to be essential, as a means of accessing 'the negativity inherent in . . . indeterminacy';[13] and if

12 Anthony Iles drew my attention to the film in a paper presented at Historical Materialism 2024, 'Plastic Givens: Speculation, Antagonism and Recursion in Uncompleted Work with Marina'.

13 Marina Vishmidt, 'Indifferent Agent: Speculation as a Mode of Production in Art and Capital', in *Economy: Art, Production and the*

thought occurs in this space where 'one institution transits as if whole and unharmed' into another institution, to produce either bizarre juxtapositions (women *become* the plates they clean), or a simple disclosure of dependence – *if this is how Marina's critical theory works*, then all levels of the analysis operate on one another, and recursivity is the means to keep moving through them without setting up one as the 'truth' of the others: a critical theory *of* movement as a theory of *mis*use, whether of NYC fare gates, Marxist-feminist theory, kitchen hatches, reproductive labour or the institutionalised traditions of conceptual art. If you 'collapse all the mediations together . . . brutally, they come out the more sharply as they decompress under the eye'. Marina always loved a film by the German feminist artist Margaret Raspé, *The Sadist Whips the Obviously Innocent* (1971), and wrote about it repeatedly, for the last time just two months before she died.[14] There, the artist intrepidly straps a camera to her head and then uses an electric whisk to beat up some cream – an early first-person shooter. There was perhaps some projective identification here: a mutual love of mixing things up.

In fact, it was in a text about Raspé's film that Marina wrote about 'infrastructure' at length for the first time: 'Reproduction as axiom,' she proposed there, sarcastically: 'Once we get the infrastructure – or, as the jargon has it, "the means of not dying" – right, then our work here is done.'[15] That was in early 2015, in a lecture initially prepared for the experimental poetry magazine *Materials*. Several lines of critical inquiry here click into place for

Subject in the Twenty-First Century, edited by Angela Dimitrakaki and Kirsten Lloyd, Liverpool: Liverpool University Press, 2015, 72.

14 Marina Vishmidt, 'On the Recursivity of Care', talk at the Curtis R. Priem Experimental Media and Performing Arts Center, 22 February 2024, empac.rpi.edu.

15 Vishmidt, 'A Short Introduction to Reproductive Realism'.

the first time like accessories of some merciless kitchen appliance. As the long years of (real) abstraction in the wake of the 2007–8 financial crisis gave way to its long concrete aftermath (geophysical crisis, state abandonment, proliferating discourses of resilience), a generation of artists began to use the language of Marxist-feminism – including its focus on reproduction – as an alibi for the refusal of a politics of 'critique', including of collective politics in the art field as such. At the same time, self-managed infrastructures of reproduction were increasingly depicted as a kind of utopian political horizon, elevating mere survival, the art of not dying, to the status of a political goal:

> preoccupation with 'infrastructures' defined by their flexibility and resilience depends tacitly on the idea of the present or future collapse . . . of whatever infrastructure already exists; *so that its concept of usefulness grows in appeal only by tacitly promoting the idea that our existing structure of useful labour will at any moment be subjected to irreversible devastation.*[16]

In *Speculation as a Mode of Production*, 'usefulness' was already analysed as a term immanent to the capitalist value-form, defined by the co-existence of use-value and exchange-value in the commodity. The two poles traverse one another. When art(istic autonomy) and labour arrive at a point of 'indistinction', they each 'trigger reflexive negations' in the other.[17] Infrastructure appears at the end of the book in much the same way: as a subcategory of the 'useful', a term in a relation, a hole in a thing that

16 Vishmidt, *Speculation as a Mode of Production*, 222.

17 Vishmidt, 'Indifferent Agent', 72. Marina's most extensive engagement with the concept of autonomy is in the book she co-authored with Kerstin Stakemeier, *Reproducing Autonomy: Work, Money, Crisis and Contemporary Art*, London: Mute, 2016.

it is not. On this Marxist, or more specifically 'value-theoretical', account, it follows that *if* the opposition of 'useful' infrastructures to 'abstract' critique affirms one term in the relation at the expense of the other, then theoretical vocabulary absents itself from the field of social form, in which concrete and abstract are always contradictory moments in a higher unity, the commodity. Also, political debate contracts into variations on a theme: the effort to develop radical concepts ('care', 'the useful', 'the infrastructural'), rather than to conceptualise 'radical thought' as 'counter-reification device' and 'conceptual solvent', a way of breaking concepts down and setting thought in motion.[18]

On the wall of Marina's living room in Hackney there hung a print of the Danish painter Asger Jorn's *Canard inquiétant* (The Unquiet Duck, 1959), in which Jorn famously took a kitschy twentieth-century landscape painting and then scrawled over the top of it an infantile, elephantine duck, its Goyaesque beak dripping orange-yellow gore. Like the toy donkey in Brecht's studio that wore a sign saying, 'I too must understand it,' this domestic familiar conveyed an important theoretical axiom. Infrastructure is 'mediated' by social abstraction, but the relation between these terms can itself be made into a means of composition. 'Critique' in the Jorn painting (in this case, critique as vandalism) depends on the pre-existing 'infrastructure' of the landscape painting he defaces; but this infrastructure is the medium of the critique and becomes something other than itself through its changed conditions of use.[19] Widen the historical aspect ratio and it is obvious

18 Vishmidt, 'A Short Introduction to Reproductive Realism'. 'Every object implies a tableau,' wrote Marina, in an essay on the British conceptual artist Chris Evans.

19 'Any category that seems unimpeachable in principle was never really your friend': Marina Vishmidt, 'Resilience, Or . . .', Commissioned as part of Let's Get Together and Call Ourselves an Institute, Chapter Thirteen (2018), vishmidt.memoryoftheworld.org.

that Marx's use of the Sorcerer's Apprentice parable in the commodity fetish chapter of *Capital* is already prototypical 'maintenance art' in the style pioneered by Mierle Laderman Ukeles a century later, and that the dancing broomsticks, the self-incinerating map of Claire Fontaine's *America (burnt/unburnt)*, the human ironing board of Letícia Parente's *Tarefa I*, the waste that has 'a dynamic and a personality of its own', the slave as the *instrumentum vocale* or 'speaking implement', Pierre Klossowski's 'living currency' and Margarete Raspé's half-woman half-whisk are all so many other walking, talking ways in which the infrastructures of social life can be made to tell the same story, about the ways in which abstract and concrete operate on one another, through the form of the commodity and the waste and the disorder to which that violent, speculative identity gives rise.[20]

In 2026, the language *of* infrastructure is more or less ubiquitous, though many of its end-users still believe themselves to be thinking simply about things. For 'critics' of political economy in the Marxist tradition, this only partially materialist outlook is painfully limited, insofar as it fails to see that infrastructure *speaks its own language* whether we want it to or not, an abstract language of flows and investment schedules extending into the long run, in which, famously, we are all dead. Affirmative theories of infrastructure, sometimes bruited in the artworld as a kind of 'critique of critique' – a moral economy of the 'useful' conceived as the means to survive in austere circumstances, in which criticism is set aside as a 'luxury' – falls short in this sense, because it fails to situate 'the useful' within a dialectical unity of capitalist value, a unity that is no less concrete than it is abstract.[20] But the unquiet duck who sails through infrastructural critique from its first conception is also

20 Marina Vishmidt, 'A Heteroclite Excursus into the Currency that Lives', *Open!* (2014), onlineopen.org.

a reminder that 'mediation' is not just an objective social process (the basis of 'real abstraction') but also a means of composition: a way to animate the material conditions of our social life by connecting material struggle to the practice of 'social invention', and of locating new registers of critique by making the materials move:

> Marina where are you in here? . . . the world of your objects is being exposed to an irresistible decay . . . I need your desire to move through them, across them, to animate them again, as Zoe said so truthfully about you, to join them again through the superlative medium of your being alive and knowing them and loving them and introducing them into your beautiful puzzling sentences, puzzles and jigsaws and Vision Masters and etch a sketches and toys everywhere, you my best friend, you beautiful child whose mother worked in a toy shop, you riddle.[21]

Marina was a serious critic of political economy, but she was also, always, playing, which means thinking about the ways to make things speak. The medium of her riddles was always the mediations, the disappearing walls, the frames that become what they frame, their own objects, puzzling jigsaw-like objects that disassemble themselves and then transit whole and unharmed into something else. 'If we follow a number of contemporary commentaries which attempt to place transformations in the conceptual and productive infrastructures of art along a trajectory of economic and social change,' Marina wrote in her PhD, '*then the*

21 From a letter to Marina read at her memorial in July 2024. 'Marina was a kind of animist,' observed her friend and co-author Zoe Sutherland.

axis where this change has been often situated is that of language.'[22] Infrastructural critique is about language, then, about how infrastructure speaks, about the language of the value-form but also a language of another kind, the language that comes from the collapsing and decompression of mediations under the eye, a language of the crisis of things, its syntax scraped from error and the conjugations of negation and surprise; and then about the freezing of 'radical thought' that serves as alibi for the silencing of all this, for endless reproduction of the same. It is part of the strategy of mixing things up always to conceive 'Marxism' in the theory of infrastructure as a way of thinking about the operation of the mediations as the basis of another kind of speech, a way of speaking back to things, with things, with other things, with an Etch A Sketch, in a language that loves things for their opacity. Does it hurt to say I hate care? But unless you learn to say it then the infrastructure says it for you.[23]

3.

So it starts with zines and movies and skipping turnstiles in the NYC subway, and it continues with the language of things and the collective culture of the small magazine. Throughout the period of her formation as a critical theorist, Marina remained committed to the Deleuzian concept of 'individuation', to the idea that *there is no individual* without 'a collective social context' (Paolo Virno), without the means for its formation in the form of an infrastructural

---

22 Marina Vishmidt, *Speculation as a Mode of Production in Art and Capital*, PhD submitted at Queen Mary University, 2013, 179.

23 Marina Vishmidt, 'Care in / as Fire' (2021), Feminist Art Maintenance Group statement, f-a-m.group.

common ground.[24] Her own 'collective social context' was, for many years, a loose grouping of left publishing projects on the borderline between politics and art, like the already mentioned *Mute*, its Scottish twin *Variant*, the outputs of the gallery space-cum-commons Casco and the eponymous publication of the Russian art collective Chto Delat. Marina always thought the alternative to a collective context was 'value subjectivity': non-speculative identity of subject and capital.

In the London art scene of the mid-2010s, a peculiarly distorted version of this idea began to acquire visibility in the inverted, conservative form of a theory of infrastructure. It starts with gallery directors talking anti-austerity and drinking highballs on the rooftop bar of a converted carpark in gentrifying Peckham, and it ends with private collectors with a background in supplying ordnance to the IDF refashioning themselves as trailblazers for the new, radically reproductive common sense. The doctrine that 'artists need to eat', and that the objective need for infrastructure always trumps the subjective desire for collective politics, reached its provisional endpoint on a cold morning in February 2017, amid confrontation and broken glass, with a protest outside the neo-reactionary, 'race realist' art gallery LD50, for the previous twelve months an exhibition space for many of what Marina would call the 'reproductive realists' of the London art scene.[25] Marina was there, selling 'Shut Down LD50' T-shirts at cost price outside, putting into practice her belief that the flipside of commitment to collective political antagonism is always the funfair egalitarianism that all shall

24 Paolo Virno, 'The Dismeasure of Art: An Interview with Paolo Virno', *Chto Delat* (2008), chtodelat.org; originally in *Arts in Society: Being an Artist in Post-Fordist Times*, edited by Pascal Gielen and Paul De Bruyne, Rotterdam: NAi Uitgevers, 2009.

25 Larne Abse Gogarty, 'The Art Right', *Art Monthly*, April 2017.

have prizes! She didn't skip turnstiles any more, and she no longer worked in catering, but the account of reproductive realism that threads its way through her writings on infrastructural critique – 'an infrastructural acedia, thuggishly pouting' – was always *personal* for her, in a manner that is unusual in a body of theoretical writing that otherwise always places its emphasis on the trans-individual and the collective. She arrived in London with no resources, no family network and no legal right to remain, and her distaste, bordering on disgust, for this particular 'cycle of reification' derived from its status as a travesty or obscene doubling of her beliefs, a cruel joke at the expense of the need for a collective context issuing, with mechanical inevitability, into a self-sculpting and -exculpating determinism.[26]

At the moment when the windows of LD50 were being smashed, she had recently finished the first sketch of a programme for an explicitly '*infrastructural* critique', as a successor to the conceptual art tradition of *institutional* critique formalised by Benjamin Buchloh, Andrea Fraser and others. The explanation of how she got there is inseparable from her engagement with collective magazine projects as vehicles of subject-formation, as well as with her Raspean propensity to take an electric whisk to the industrially separated discursive entities of 'politics' and 'art', but the genealogy of the concept requires us to take a step back from the reproduction/infrastructure debate in the artworld, and to explore a related post-crisis discussion in the field of communist theory:

> In times of crisis, when the ratio of waged to unwaged starts to tilt negatively, reproduction becomes the political battleground, if only through sheer force of numbers of people who can't get access to a wage, as well as the

26 Vishmidt, 'A Short Introduction to Reproductive Realism'.

> important category of the 'working poor' who have to rely on benefits.[27]

The blockade of the Port of Oakland in September 2011 under the rubric of a 'General Strike' revived a discussion of logistics, technology and capitalist infrastructure first introduced into anarchist and communist debates some years before by the acts of sabotage at the centre of the case of the Tarnac 9. At the same time, Marxist-feminist discussions around the 'gender relation' also began to 'tilt negatively', a movement memorably encapsulated in a response by Maya Gonzalez and Jeanne Neaton in the third issue of the journal *Endnotes* to Silvia Federici's call for feminists to 'reclaim the house as a center of collective life', that 'we do consider this possibility worse than death'.[28] The intensity of those debates, and the rapidity with which they ran up against the limits of their own abstractions, is captured by some introductory remarks of Marina's in a lecture, 'Reproduction of What?', delivered in Banff in 2014. 'Two years ago,' she wrote then,

> I took the stance that a focus on reproduction, in the ways the Italian workerist and post-workerist marxist feminists defined it, was still in and of itself a radical challenge to the system of gendered abjection and exploitation that constituted the reproduction of capital and its social system. Even then however, I was beginning to understand that a further layer of abstraction was needed, one which saw gender as a form to be abolished alongside the form of value: a toxic mediation that the process of communisation would have to

27 Marina Vishmidt, 'Human Capital or Toxic Asset: After the Wage', *Mute*, 2011, metamute.org.

28 Endnotes, 'The Logic of Gender: On the separation of spheres and the process of abjection', *Endnotes*, 3 (2013), endnotes.org.uk.

> confront and overcome for the communist project to have any hope of succeeding. This maximalist horizon, the immanence of feminism to communism posed in this way, was appealing. These days I am less convinced that the category of abolition taken on its own, no less than the category of reproduction, are adequate responses to the feminist problematic, or to the social and ecological crisis in which we encounter it.[29]

Marina's participation in these discussions, signally at a conference on the concept of 'subsumption' in Bilbao in 2014, was a major influence on the terms of her own approach, beginning in the mid-2000s, to the political claims and histories of institutional critique. While her own contribution to the Bilbao event took the form of a mapping exercise, in which abolitionist proposals within feminism and Black radicalism were examined together, the discussion around 'subsumption' (of labour, life, of infrastructure under capital) seemed, to her, to be unhelpfully, abstractly metaphysical.[30] Its sterility was registered by the movement of many of the participants in the debate towards other, more practical forms of activity:

> we are precipitated into rather 'theological' problematics of immanence and transcendence; into questions of whether the mode of production has any 'outside'; into visions of the future as a completely contentless blank slate – for if

29 Marina Vishmidt, 'Reproduction of What?: On Reproduction in an Extra-Systemic Sense', keynote at the Marxist Literary Group Summer Institute on Culture and Society, 2014.

30 Marina Vishmidt, 'The Paradox of Self-Abolition: A Mapping Exercise', *May* 10 (16); see also her text in *Abolishing Capitalist Totality: What Is to Be Done under Real Subsumption?*, edited by Anthony Iles and Mattin, Colchester: Minor Compositions, 2026.

> everything really is to be at stake, then what lies beyond can only be nothing.[31]

That last passage is from an article on infrastructure by *Endnotes*, first published in 2015, focused on the eternal return of elementary metaphysical questions in debates about communism in which 'communisation' can only be perceived as a pure event: a rupture with everything that is knowable or sayable within the material conditions of capitalist social life. Marina's response to its criticisms was characteristically non-intuitive. Rather than reading in it a *legitimation* of the knowable and sayable institutions of contemporary art, she instead recognised, 'transversally', that the remarks apply with near perfect homological exactitude to Andrea Fraser's assertion, at the end of her important 'From the Critique of Institutions to an Institution of Critique' (2005), that 'we cannot exist outside the field of art, at least not as artists, critics, curators, etc.'.[32] And this becomes the move with which an explicitly 'infrastructural critique' is inaugurated: the totalisation of the institution of art and the totalisation of abolition (of art as well as all other social institutions) are folded into one another, so that each becomes a ground that also feels like a container. The diagnosis of an end is folded back into a beginning, the insights of communist theory transiting as if whole and unharmed into another institution, the institution of art; each a rabbit to the other's duck.[33] Just as for *Endnotes*, infrastructure interrupts the 'false totalization' of theories of subsumption under the heading

31 The original publication was Endnotes, 'Error', *Bad Feelings*, London: Bookworks, 2015; the quote comes from the more extensive version, 'Error', *Endnotes* 5 (2019), 132.

32 Fraser, 'From the Critique of Institutions to an Institution of Critique'.

33 As per the famous reversible figure in Wittgenstein's *Philosophical Investigation*.

of 'error', infrastructure becomes, for Marina, a means of challenging the 'false totalizations' of institutional critique in the field of contemporary art.

A year after the appearance of the *Endnotes* piece, a month after the protest that shut down LD50, Marina's short essay 'Between Not Everything and Not Nothing: Cuts Towards Infrastructural Critique' argued, with explicit reference to the *Endnotes* text, that it is 'infrastructure's transitive character – between the material and the possible, between machines and working drawings, between cognitive maps and what is pictured on them – that enables it to ask political questions that can no longer be replied to in the abstract, with the false totalizations of rejection or complicity'.[34] Infrastructure now appears in her writing as a figure of recursivity and as a response to the potentially theological preoccupation of institutional critique with the question of outsides. The specific significance of its displacement from the *Endnotes* piece into an argument about *institutional* critique rests in turn on two distinct ironies. The first is the identification of the loop I've already mentioned, between the false totalisation of art and the false totalisation of the discourse of its abolition. The second is that Marina's first definition of infrastructure *is still a definition of reproduction*: infrastructure, like reproductive labour, is 'that which repeats'. The 'reproductive aspect of infrastructure, however, has to retain an openness to the "temporal cut", which undoes crystallizations and institutions in the attempt to realize the desires that were the initial impetus for their establishment'. The art institution appears as something requiring infrastructure to be reproduced, and its infrastructure appears as

34 Marina Vishmidt, 'Between Everything and Not Nothing: Cuts Towards Infrastructural Critique', in *Former West: Art and the Contemporary after 1989*, edited by Maria Hlavadjova and Simon Sheikh, Cambridge: MIT Press, 2017.

something that repeats, returning us, by means of another conceptual loop, to the earlier critique of gender as 'toxic mediation' and as a 'form to be abolished'. The concept recurs and the conditions of is recurrence are *critical*, allowing Marina to deal with infrastructure in the same way that she dealt with reproduction itself in *Speculation as a Mode of Production*, by means of a speculative identification in which the endpoint of analysis loops back to its beginning, and negativity is preserved in spite of and against the lures of abstract totalisation.[35] The aim is to develop a negativity that is immanent to the object itself, that is not abstract and does not require theological problematics of transcendence, the apophatic or abstract idea that the only way to negate 'what is' is to go beyond, as per the Lucio Fulci movie, by means of a gesture of abolition about which it is impossible to say anything except that it is nothing that we can know or be, because to do so would only prove that we are 'still inside', irrespective of whether the inside in question is capitalism or the institution of art – institutions whose speculative identity Marina had already established. The *origins* of this thinking in political and communist debates clarifies the *purpose* of its method. This is a contribution at the level of theory that is deeply concerned with the problem of practice, and its apparent sophistication is deeply rooted in the simple desire to make sure that 'an angry, loving detachment from what keeps us running in place', a negativity without end, is itself an endless source of movement: that it does not pass over into the paralytic meta-stable abstractions of a 'transgressive negativity' that evacuates all speculative relationship to the real and the concrete. What 'repeats is not without

35 'Thus we can propose that speculation as a mode of production also implies a becoming-speculative of reproduction', *Speculation as a Mode of Production*, IX.

difference'.[36] Marina Vishmidt's 'materialist theory of conditions' or infrastructural critique participates as if by an optical illusion in several conversations at once, depending on how you look at it, and the recursive negativity that allows it to do this, to make negativity differential and immanent to its own concepts and objects, is her own contribution to the tendency she once noted, 'vastly different as their apparatus of reference is', in the respective projects of Fred Moten and Ray Brassier: 'Far from filling abolition with a positive epistemic or social content, this dwelling on nothingness seems rather to point to the lived experience of negativity as mediation with rather than cancellation of "the world".'[37]

The final phase of Marina's programme of infrastructural critique can be picked up in late 2021:

> My work as a theorist or a writer, an analyst of contemporary culture with a focus on contemporary art from a marxist, feminist, internationalist and Black studies perspective, *from the labor perspective, basically*, has not just been informed, but in a lot of ways been eclipsed by ... labour struggles and their political and strategic implications ... I feel like they set not just the infrastructural but the theoretical conditions for this activity in an absolute way, as they do for a lot of my friends and comrades.[38]

---

36 An allusion to Gilles Deleuze, *Difference and Repetition*, translated by Paul Patton, London: Continuum, 1994. Reproduction of conditions vis-à-vis conditions of reproduction form yet another loop: Deleuze's account of repetition as difference becomes a means of approaching it dynamically.

37 Marina Vishmidt, 'Procedures of Abolition: and Several Paradoxes They Throw Up', in *Abolishing Capitalist Totality*.

38 Marina Vishmidt and Danny Hayward, 'Materialities Shaped by Divisions', *Arts of the Working Class*, 32 (2024), 30, vishmidt.memoryoftheworld.org.

Here, Marina, at this time recovering from a cancer-related injury exacerbated by the failure of the UK health system during the pandemic, argues that 'labour struggles ... set ... the infrastructural conditions ... in an absolute way'. The art institution is to be seen as 'a historical and contingent nexus of material conditions amenable to rearrangement *through struggle*', and critique is a 'social practice that will not suffer but actually benefit from those institutions [those in which the critic works] being blown sky-high'.[39]

The transition is itself a result, something posited, to use the Hegelian language, by the cannibalistic, world-ending fury of capitalist social relations as she experienced it: 'in a social order held together by the bones of those who didn't survive it, cancer can act as a lenticular tool to hold our fates in high resolution'.[40] But it also introduces a break between *Speculation as a Mode of Production* and *Infrastructural Critique*, because, while the first is a theoretical work rooted in Marxist critique of political economy, the second becomes, under historical and bodily duress, an interventionist project oriented towards and discursively participating in struggle itself, or, to persist in Hegelian jargon, an element of struggle reflecting on itself. Infrastructural critique as 'materialist theory of conditions' (of reproduction) upends a contemplative, Kantian philosophical idiom to supply its readers with means for mobile or situational thinking about material possibilities and impossibilities, across the locations and institutional sites of the artworld and its 'edges', even as it refuses to

39 The first of these formulations can be found in Chapter 1 of this book, but both occurred originally in '"Only as Self-Relating Negativity", Infrastructure and Critique', *Journal of Science and Technology of the Arts*, 13, 3 (2022), 14, 17.

40 Marina Vishmidt, review of Anne Boyer's *The Undying*, *Artforum*, 58, 4 (2019), artforum.com.

establish reproduction as horizon or final ground.[41] The combinatorial metaphor, of 'material conditions amenable to *rearrangement* through struggle', reinforces this approach at the same time as it suggests, as does the language of 'bracketing' ('my friends and comrades . . . have spent years developing a set of scholarly or theoretical interests and have either bracketed them or recontextualised them in the constant process of collective struggle'), a pragmatic disposition towards political, theoretical or conceptual vocabularies, including Marina's own.[42] Accompanying this shift, we see something like a historical transition in the artworks themselves: away from the 'bohemianism of evasion' highlighted in 'Cuts Towards Infrastructural Critique', and towards 'emphatic solidarity of condition' in the work of Carolyn Lazard, Cameron Rowland, Anna Engelhardt and, perhaps most explicitly in this case, since their work was first introduced as an example of the former tendency, Pilvi Takala. What began as a critique of the doctrine of the 'useful' becomes, through commitment to subjective transformation within the collective social context, a critical theory of *mis*use, individuated out of its material conditions, ambidextrous between the perspectives of reproduction and abolition, suspicious of false totalisations, and dedicated to the principle that all should have prizes.

4.

'Reversible figures', we read in Wikipedia, 'are visual forms that create ambiguity by exploiting graphical similarities and other properties of visual system interpretation between two or more

41 Andreas Petrossiants, 'Inside and Out: The Edges to Critique', *e-flux journal*, 110 (2020), e-flux.com.

42 Vishmidt and Hayward, 'Materialities Shaped by Divisions', 30.

distinct image forms.' To think in reversible figures means to think under the sign of contingency, indexicality, unstable reference and recursion, making negation into a property of the object itself rather than a decree echoing hollowly from its outside. 'Infrastructural critique' is also a reversible figure – perhaps deliberately a reversible figure in this sense. Its construction is chiasmic. Critique of infrastructure requires infrastructure of critique and vice versa, and the recursivity of this formulation picks up a theme that runs throughout Marina's work on art, finance and philosophy, in her engagement with Donald Mackenzie's book *An Engine not a Camera* and her years-long fascination with Benjamin's dream allegory in which he stands in front of and is located within a 'map of hell' (alluded to, perhaps, in the Channels film-essay), as well as her essay on the Gwion Gwion paintings as 'wholly indexical in an absorption of the mark in the process of marking'.[43] The role of indexical self-reference as a disrupter ('This sentence is not true') suggests a critique (of art) by means of infrastructure or the artistic criticism of infrastructure, depending on how you look at it: it is an intervention in several different discussions at once, in an intellectual culture in which the participants of each are habitually inclined to remain oblivious of one another, to the point of making their own special versions of the argument that there is no outside of art, of life, of revolutionary politics. As a way of participating in debates, the method itself recalls a term from the linguistics of Roman Jakobson, the 'shifter',

43 Donald Mackenzie, *An Engine not a Camera: How Financial Models Shape Markets*, Cambridge: MIT Press, 2006; Walter Benjamin, 'Diary Entries, 1936', 6 March 1938, in *Walter Benjamin: Selected Writings, Volume 3, 1935–1938*, edited by Howard Eiland and Michael W. Jennings, Cambridge: Harvard University Press, 2002, 335–6; Marina Vishmidt, 'The Fable of the Bacteria', *Allegory of the Cave Painting*, edited by Mihnea Mircan and Vincent W. J. van Gerven Oei, Milan: Mousse Publishing.

a linguistic element whose reference changes depending on its (collective social) context – a term that might serve as a metaphor for a mode of intervention based on transiting as if whole and unharmed from one institution into another, a rabbit-duck in the fields of aesthetics and politics, in search of experimental practice.[44]

This fascination with reference systems as elements of aesthetic politics, and also simply of politics, since the distinction between the two domains is inane, connects Marina's work on infrastructural critique to one final current of her research in the years before her death. In her 2020 *Radical Philosophy* essay 'Bodies in Space', she argues against the uptake in contemporary political jargon of the language of 'bodies' as the preferred locution for the individual or person, insisting that this was evidence of 'an *anti-abstracting* desire' that blocks attempts 'to get a handle on what other bodies are possible'.[45] Judith Butler's claims in their theory of 'performative assembly' for the political power of the 'fragile, isolated, and suffering body' – here interestingly redolent of the needy, self-isolating body of the reproductive realists – is objected to, as an apparent materialism concealing a preference for simple abstractions. 'Preconditions' cannot be dispensed with: the attempt to do so collapses the levels of realism *as representation* and realism *as reference to the conditions of that representation*, as well as of infrastructure *of aesthetics* and aesthetics *of infrastructure*, not now in the manner of Raspé's whisk but in a

44 See the entry on 'Shifter' at nosubject.com. Marina was also deeply interested in the idea of the ruin, the ruin as allegory, the object that in suffering its own entropic decay becomes at the same time a representation of something other than itself, and through being itself changes what it represents, a problem she wrote about most explicitly in her essay on the Australian cave paintings.

45 Marina Vishmidt, 'Bodies in Space: On the ends of vulnerability', *Radical Philosophy*, 208 (2020), 42.

gesture that disavows the existence of mediation in the first place.[46]

In fact, it might be suggested that the 'Bodies in Space' article is the negative component of infrastructural critique, insofar as the 'formalistic' theory of politics it criticises, focused on the ethical claims of the individual body, is another name for political theory *minus* infrastructure, the attempt to think a politics of the self without the recursive reference to its own 'trans-individual' and material conditions which are the basis of interruption, blockage, antagonism and change. This claim, which is the most developed version of an argument against individualising assumptions masquerading as radical politics that runs throughout Marina's interventions in contemporary art discourse, brings us back, as does the conclusion of the essay, to the limitations of institutional critique: 'The only mediation whose presence is still desirable' in Butler's theory, Marina notes in passing, is the mediation of 'the art institution' itself.[47]

Approaching a conclusion means looping back one last time. At the beginning of her 2022 Arnheim lecture 'From Speculation to Infrastructure', which is now the opening of this book, Marina traces her interest in recursivity and the speculative identity of *production* and *conditions for production* to her early engagement with feminist zine culture during the mid-to-late 1990s. Of the author of those early zines, she said a few years earlier, 'this was someone who thought everything was stupid – regular culture, zine culture, all milieus were dumb and rotten, so I made fun of everything there was except for what filled me with respect due to my inability to understand it'. She also wrote that what drew her to DIY culture in the first place was 'the idea of

46 Marina Vishmidt et al., 'Realism Today?', *ARTMargins*, 7, 1 (2018), 58–82.

47 Vishmidt, 'Bodies in Space', 41.

friendship' as trans-individuation: 'friendship that resonates across time and space in love and fascination'.[48]

The contradicted starting points pile up like plates in a sink, like zines in a dorm, like anti-fascist T-shirts on a trestle table outside a fascist cultural space. 'The speculative proposition,' Marina writes, in a theoretical text on method from 2019, 'constantly poses and withdraws meaning, but all the withdrawn meanings pile up, probably in an ungainly fashion, and their interactions are unforeseeable.'[49] She always treated divisions between the academy, the artworld and radical political theory as if they were one DIY or zine culture in which negativity is the container and love and fascination the ground, as contingent borders amenable to rearrangement through struggle, as reversible figures and rabbit-ducks and paintings you can walk into.

What distinguishes her late 'materialist theory of conditions' from other works in which 'infrastructure' is a theme is a fundamental commitment to theory, to the practice of conceptual abstraction, *as a means of movement*. 'Infrastructure is what enables,' wrote Marina in 2020, 'that is the baseline';[50] and while that too simple thesis is obviously contradicted in many other places in her thinking, the assertion still conveys an emotional and intellectual truth. In a period in which the left has been split continually by global political events, and the institutions of art have revealed themselves not even as infrastructures, but simply

48 Marina Vishmidt, talk given at Non-Threatening Theatre, June 2014; Marina Vishmidt, talk given at *Towards a Transindividual Self* launch event, Archive Books, 12 January 2024.

49 Marina Vishmidt, 'Art, Value, Subjects, Reasons. Some Aspects of Speculation as Production', in *Aesthetics of Equivalence*, edited by Simon Baier and Markus Klammer, Berlin: August Verlag, 2023, 113.

50 Marina Vishmidt and Andreas Petrossiants, 'Spaces of Speculation: Movement Politics in the Infrastructure', Historical Materialism blog, 14 November 2020, historicalmaterialism.org.

as instruments of oppression, infrastructural critique defines a project that is *practical*, *materialist*, *scalable in both directions* and always oriented to alliances that cut across sectoral boundaries and the hypostatised levels of the represented and the real. Its negative dimensions outline a kind of negative space, an immanent expansion of possibility through recursive refusal of ultimate grounds. *Institutional* critique is rejected because of its argument that it is impossible to get outside art. (Complete) real subsumption is rejected because it turns abstraction into a means of immobilisation. In the 'Bodies in Space' article discussed previously, the rejection of the concept of 'bodies' in theoretical discourse appears to be differently motivated – and yet the conclusion is almost exactly the same:

> Recognition becomes the sole claim to amelioration possible to articulate here, since no other collective power, no form of social invention is conceivable, only relentless exposure (to harm, to one another) and the inescapability of this kind of life, lived in these same circumstances. This is a surplus population whose only subjectivity is its 'surplus-ness'; an actualised internalisation of the capital relation that demands recognition, and asks for counter-praxis.[51]

'The inescapability of this kind of life' establishes the basic motif of her work in the form of an inversion. Beyond its individual theses and the currency of the examples on which it draws, Marina's project of infrastructural critique can be read as a way of thinking art, social institutions and the limitation of the fragile, isolated individual body from the perspective of their escape, not now into some ineffable outside but *into one another* through the recursive movement of the book's central categories, of

51 Vishmidt, 'Bodies in Space', 45.

reproduction, speculation and negativity, played out at the level of the infrastructure on all of its many scales. 'I have always been investigating', Marina wrote in 2018, 'the desire for political effect, the desire for politics, basically ... and what kinds of subjectivities that generates.'[52]

And, with this, we find ourselves back at the NYC subway station one last time. This is a book that appears to be about materialist analysis of things, 'infrastructures', conditions we intuitively perceive as existing out of scale with our own lives, as figures of the fixed and the immovable and of the massive inescapable conditions of our existence, and yet the fundamental problem that is present on every single page of Marina's work on infrastructural critique is the problem of how to appropriate the resources of art, infrastructure and philosophy *for us* – to turn the terms of the conclusion to 'Bodies in Space' upside down – as collective power, as forms of social invention for a life lived in different circumstances, as an end to relentless exposure to harm, which does not 'ask for' counter-practice, but *offers* it. So it starts with desire, in other words, with a few tiny nicks or cuts, and in the end it loops back to the first, endless repetition in difference of the collective decision to jump.

Danny Hayward

52 Marina Vishmidt, talk on 'What Is to Be Done under Real Subsumption' panel, Historical Materialism conference, November 2018.

Part I.

Foundations

1.

Speculative Infrastructures

Conditions of possibility

From the beginning of my involvement in the field of art and cultural production, whether I was practising as an academic, a writer, an organiser, or an editor, my focus has always been, in one way or another, on conditions of possibility, whether those conditions are considered formal, social, economic, historical or ontological. These conditions of possibility include the existence and allowances of a demarcated field of practice, as well as, self-reflexively, or perhaps paradoxically, the practices that transpire in that field. Throughout all of my work, I have always wanted to know the conditions of legibility for practices to register in a field even when they might originate from elsewhere, and how practices originating in that field can work transversally or away from its demarcated boundaries. So conditions for and in a field, but also the composition of that field, along the vectors of objective and subjective determination by race, class, gender and so forth.

In other words, since before the beginning, my experience and thus my understanding of culture has been collective, with the social and personal dimensions always embedded in the conceptual. Because my entry to participation was, at first, in zine culture, which was very much defined by riot grrrl, punk and infinite configurations of both projects and structures that were DIY, the artistic and political, material and method, were co-constitutive; the milieu in its positioning was defined by antagonism, not just politically on specific issues in a right-wing cultural environment, but towards the modes of individualised celebrity and mystified creativity typical of mainstream culture. Thus, it was always clear that the ways of organising artistic production were as critical and political as anything that could be isolated as a work or as a product, and, in fact, the distinctions between these, which can also be read along the process/product binary, were always contingent matters of practice and proximity.

So this was the 1990s, obviously, the last moment in capitalist modernity, especially in the West, or the imperial/colonial rich world, when something like a self-sustaining and oppositional underground culture could be said to exist. And yet, even then, the principles and practicalities of separation from what was at the time called the 'mainstream' were starting to break down – a process that perhaps culminates in the contemporary obsolescence of the concept of 'selling out', in terms of the accompanying structure of feeling no less than the economic agenda of rugged independence it represented. Of course, many things are obvious now that would have been obvious to many also at the time: that is, as a dissident cultural milieu in the US, it was a sphere of privilege, or, in a more materialist vocabulary, of 'resource advantage'. Predominantly white and English-speaking, it thus exerted a disproportionate cultural influence even as a reference or a model of 'underground' and independent musical, publishing and artistic practice. And gender was a much more visible battle than other group identifiers ascribed for oppression and exploitation – at least within the zine milieu. Certainly, there were many other milieus in the 'underground' (you only need to think of the Detroit techno collective Underground Resistance), so it's important to come to this as only one instance of an antagonistic/self-sufficient cultural logic, again, both in terms of structure and composition. Nor do I mean to assert that this is a logic that is extinct or has been made extinct by social media platforms and their powers of capital and attention concentration and fragmentation. Funded, unfunded, less-funded, variably funded – vestiges of DIY culture continue to exist, especially in poetry and artist publishing, to take some obvious examples, though the taboo of 'selling out' is perhaps less generalised across these cultures, at least in a North American–European context.

Conditions of speculation

This very contained flashback furnishes a backdrop for explaining what I have come to refer to as infrastructural critique. In my approach, attention to infrastructure is inseparable from the attempt to develop a materialist theory of 'conditions'. This means the material conditions of the institution's reproduction, both in and beyond the art field. We need a theory that doesn't rely on idealist philosophical paradigms and yet can simultaneously attend to the so-called historical and social ontology of art. Beyond this, such a theory needs to engage with the space of social struggle and organising, the field of work, and everything that the field conceals or excludes, both within and beyond its own institutional environment. At its far limit, it should also be able to deal with questions of social abstraction, which, as I will argue throughout this book, also means with colonialism and race.

For me, these connections emerged organically, in the course of my writing and teaching and through reflection on the relations between my practical and intellectual concerns. In the years I was preparing this work, in my academic job, I was pursing my abiding concern with artistic labour and the politics of its 'exceptionality' via a Master's programme in 'culture industry', which both inhabited and turned inside out the genre of the 'cultural and creative industries': a managerial formation on offer under similar labels across the field of higher education. In class, we would spend a lot of time discussing divergences between success ideology and empirical failure, and how part of the systemic character of that failure is the erosion of social institutions like the welfare state or global trends of financialisation, underdevelopment, wage arbitrage and industries of extraction from dispossession of land to the harvesting of data. We would also talk about the infrastructures of psychic extraction, about individualisation of responsibility, or blame, for economic failure perceived as personal failure – inability to sufficiently leverage or mobilise your own human and social capital – and about the (ostensible) impossibility of collective action in an industry driven by personal branding, unless that action can itself be branded.

As we investigated the 'exceptionality' of artistic labour – the idea that such labour is constitutively distinct from labour of other kinds, including wage labour – our conversations would often return to the conditions of the field: its infrastructure. And, over time, these discussions compelled a shift in my thinking, from a notion of critique that called on a certain discourse or performance of citizenship – what we could call, essentially, a discourse of institutional *accountability* – to one that took a more 'immanent' view on the means of production of the institution or its conditions of possibility: a shift from institutional to infrastructural critique. Of course, an institution can be a type of infrastructure, but the point is to move from a standpoint that takes the institution as its horizon to one which takes the institution as a historical and contingent nexus of material conditions, amenable to rearrangement through struggle and different forms of inhabitation and dispersal. As I tried to examine the various levels at which infrastructure operates in this analysis, I also came to ask how infrastructures repeat across scales, as well as how the speculative force of aesthetics can clarify, open up and repurpose these infrastructures in investigative and/or 'transversal' political situations, or dis-appropriate them or their constituent parts for other ends.[1]

As its most basic move, the shift from institutional critique to infrastructural critique has to decide whether the horizon that critique aims for in the space of art as a 'space of permissible critique' is the institution or the social (and geophysical) world.[2] My first answer is to say 'surely, it's both', but also to designate the ways in which each term folds into the other, meaning that infrastructural critique, as I conceive it, deals with infrastructure *both within and beyond art*, but does not take a static view on the relevant scales and boundaries. This implies a refusal of the metonymic move that simply treats art as a microcosm of social reality, while also insisting on specificity – the specificity of particular social spaces with particular material possibilities or 'affordances'. My approach is always to think strategically. There needs to be a double focus on infrastructure both in and beyond institutions. This entails zeroing in on their conditions of reproduction, and drawing speculative lines of solidarity from there. As Andreas Petrossiants has written, 'the terms – artist, tenant, worker – aren't specific classes but, rather, forms of exploitation or forms of (re) production that can be overcome by creating solidarity networks across occupation, across fields, across income levels'.[3]

1 For a first approach to 'transversality', see Félix Guattari, *Molecular Revolution: Psychiatry and Politics*, translated by Rosemary Sheed, London: Penguin, 1984.

2 Hannah Black, 'The Identity Artist and the Identity Critic', *Artforum*, 54, 10 (Summer 2016), artforum.com.

3 Andreas Petrossiants, in *Diversity of Aesthetics*, vol. I, *Inside and Outside: Infrastructures of Critique*, edited by Andreas Petrossiants and Jose Rosales, New York: Emily Harvey Foundation, 35.

Conditions of struggle

This open-ended approach to infrastructure can also be thought of as speculative. Over the past years of critically engaged participation in the sphere of activity that has, until recently, been neutrally known as 'contemporary art', I have been developing a constellation of ideas that speak about the imbrication of art with political and economic forces in the disaster capitalism of our era, from the standpoint of the production of subjectivity and labour. I came to call this constellation 'speculation as a mode of production'. In my 2018 book of that title, I explored art and financial capitalism as two institutions of contemporary life that deploy a surplus of uncertainty – speculation, risk – to ground their claims on value.[4] At the same time, I was interested to underline how both are mechanisms of making labour 'disappear' using the spells of creativity, freedom and self-investment.

With the simultaneous expansion of finance *and* art in the speculative mode of production, the boundaries between art and labour become indistinct: the labourer becomes an entrepreneur, creatively speculating on their 'human capital', and the artist becomes a prototype for the 'post-Fordist' labourer.[5] But, with this hypothesis of speculative identity, a contrary proposition emerges: speculative identity is also a *non-identity* in the sense defined by Theodor W. Adorno, in the sense that identity thinking must be thought against itself and yet thought cannot help but identify.[6] *Speculative identity is both sameness and difference.*

4 Marina Vishmidt, *Speculation as a Mode of Production: Forms of Value-Subjectivity in Art and Capital*, Leiden: Brill, 2018.

5 Vishmidt, *Speculation as a Mode of Production*, X, 21, 25.

6 Theodor W. Adorno, *Negative Dialectics*, translated by E. B. Ashton, New York: Seabury Press, 1973, 143ff; see also Marina Vishmidt, 'The Hard Labour of Speculation: Shaping a Reflection on Methods', *MaHKUscript: Journal of Fine Art Research*, 3, 1, 1–8.

This experience of difference can then recursively enter into the construction of a critical approach that receives its orientation from non-identity and hence strives to remain speculative at the level of concepts as well as practical intervention.

In all of my work, I try to keep coming back to categories as ways of staking out relations of antagonism, rather than categories as fixed classes of things, or identities. This comes back to 'non-identity' as a form of social experience, and the wish to deflect the reification of boundaries in political and artistic praxis. I remain committed to the notion that capitalism is the total enemy (relation) that incorporates and generates all others, speaking and thinking historically and systematically rather than mythically or ontologically. Since capital totalises and separates, as part of its own valorisation and the suppression of the life of everything else, what this means is that we have to fight in specificity, as Black queer feminist socialist movements have shown from the 1970s right up to the present.[7] It's necessary to know what is based in a common world, and what is a specific fight based on how that world has identified and subjugated you, and where struggles overlap or diverge.[8] So when saying that capitalism is the total enemy, what that has to mean is that capitalism = anti-Black exterminism, capitalism = misogyny, capitalism = ecological collapse. None of these are incidental or simply included in a higher term, *they are synonyms*, and it's obtuse to try to separate them, logically or empirically.

This approach to categories governs my approach both to speculation as a mode of production and infrastructural critique.

---

7 See Combahee River Collective, *The Combahee River Collective Statement*, blackpast.org.

8 Marina Vishmidt, 'Lights, Camera, Now Time!: Polly II, Plan for a Revolution in the Docklands', *Mousse*, 7 October 2024, moussemagazine.it.

In the period in which the focal point of my research shifted from the former to the latter, the forms of speculative finance that we talked about in class have developed – have been allowed to develop – to a point where they are functionally insulated from catastrophic social and ecological tendencies that they have institutionalised, rewarded and found ways to profit from for a long time. The institutions of art have often served as consensus-building mechanisms in this totality, structurally and ideologically laundering the imperative to extract profit and offering avenues of representation of alterity that remain notional on the whole so far as their own conditions of possibility are not at stake. For the time being, the reflective shimmer of a politically radicalised art necessarily feeds off what it critiques, until, I would propose, it can learn to operate transversally with struggles in the infrastructure – both in the arts and elsewhere. Ultimately, this may imply an infrastructural vision that will make art as it is currently practised impossible, because both capitalism and the autonomy it grants to art would have disappeared into the black hole opened up by our present situation and the historical movements to overcome it.

This moment may seem a long way off. The following chapters approach it by means of a dialectical and non-exhaustive approach, suspicious of theoretical closures or inflations of all kinds, but guided by the wager that we need to be thinking about infrastructure full stop, in all areas of our counter-planning and organising, and that the 'speculative' space of art is one space among others where that thinking needs to happen. It is the institution's commitment to artistic autonomy that can be used to expose its universal complicity, so to speak, but this is secondary: the priority is the situation of collective rebellion that is capable of turning the hard division between inside and out into a chalk drawing on the pavement around the defunct institution, and taking it as a space for our 'plans', as Fred Moten and

Stefano Harney might say.[9] That is, in many ways, the baseline of this book.

Speculative infrastructures

Having set the scene, I'd now like to move anti-clockwise, at least in terms of Marx's plotting of a movement from the abstract to the concrete, to a more in-depth exploration of what I mean in working with the concepts of 'speculation' and 'infrastructure' as what I call 'experimental totalisations'.

Initially, I take speculation in its character as a powerful logic of contemporary life whose key instantiations are art and finance. Both are premised on the power of contingency, the fluidity of temporality and experimentation with the creation (and capitalisation) of possible worlds. Artistic autonomy, the 'self-legislation' of the space of art, was once and often still is seen as the freedom to speculate wildly on material and social possibilities. The artist as a speculative subject is also seen as the paragon of creativity, the complete opposite of both a *Homo economicus* obsessed with balance sheets and value-added and optimising investment, and a *Homo laborans*, in Hannah Arendt's terms, which we would have to expand from her gender-deterministic framework to include those whose lives are limited by the imperative to work and to reproduce workers, in conditions where both that labour and its results are controlled and accumulated by others.[10] However, once social reality becomes speculative and opaque in its own right, risky and algorithmic, overhauled by networked markets in

9 Fred Moten and Stefano Harney, *The Undercommons: Fugitive Planning and Black Study*, Wivenhoe: Minor Compositions, 2013.

10 Hannah Arendt, *The Human Condition*, 2nd ed., Chicago: University of Chicago Press, 1958, 144ff.

everything, what becomes of the distinction between not just art and finance, but art and life? In working with these premises, the point is to develop approaches to specific artistic practices as crystals of both ownership and dispossession, with all the strategic and ontological ambiguities that cluster around both of those poles. We need to grasp the stakes of speculation as an issue for current and recent art, and to develop a transversal concept of speculation in doing so, one that departs from, but is not limited to, the infrastructures of art and finance sketched out earlier.

The subjective drive to speculation as the generation of 'new ideas' per se becomes codified as 'creativity' in the neoliberal labour market. As a consequence, creativity becomes, paradoxically, a characteristic of abstract labour, which was Marx's generic category for the social institution of wage labour in a capitalist society – 'abstract', because most labour relationships end up being indifferent to the content of the labour and are mainly used for acquiring money to live, or, if you are a capitalist or entrepreneur, to accumulate or speculate with. I argue that such a shift heralds the conversion of the fetishised creativity of art into a pre-eminent instance of speculation as a mode of production, since art becomes no longer just a commodity in the market or a gratuitous activity but increasingly a tool of socialisation into the speculative mode and an accessory to the re-valorisation of land and the displacement of populations, as in the well-known link between art venues and gentrification.[11] It thus takes on a new instrumentality relative to the dialectic of autonomy and heteronomy assigned to art by Marxist critics such as Adorno. At the same time, this is an instrumentality which in turn speculates *with* the autonomy and creative

11 To take one example from among many: Anthony Iles and Josephine Berry Slater, *No Room to Move: Radical Art and the Regenerate City*, London: Mute Publishing, 2012.

freedom assigned specifically to art in an unfree society in order to ground both its ethical claims and its financial value, depending on the context.

From being hypothetically separate from the economy, the artist becomes a creative tasked with diligently optimising their quantified self, an increasingly abject and coercive situation, and the two senses of speculation – artistic thinking and financial operations – converge, something we have observed not just in the more familiar critical descriptions of the artist as entrepreneurial subject par excellence, but also in more recent developments such as crypto-art and NFTs, where the moments of artistic creation and market valorisation can no longer be kept apart, and neither can coercion and speculation in a stagnant, crisis-prone economy (freedom of finance, subjugation of labour). Here, a dependency and a resonance emerge between the open-ended processes of speculative thought and the profit-driven (or, in cybernetic terms, homeostatic) world of financial speculation. At the same time, however, we need to retain another sense of speculation, as the commitment to experimentation and non-utility, for social and political as well as aesthetic and cognitive reasons. As Henk Slager notes, 'From an artistic perspective, it seems essential to start investigating the following methodological question: how could we engage in that assignment of reconsidering and revealing speculation in order to arrive at novel panoramas and "not-yet-known-knowledge"?'[12] We also can think here of speculative philosophical propositions such as G. W. F. Hegel's speculative logic, Adorno's already mentioned concept of non-identity, or Denise Ferreira da Silva's notion of 'difference without separability' as some

12 Henk Slager, 'Whatever Speculation', *MaHKUscript Journal of Fine Art Research*, 3, 1 (2019).

conceptual and methodological touchstones.[13] When we work with these kinds of models, we can contextualise artworks in their conditions of production and exchange in such a way as to be able to see artistic practices and materials in the social relations and histories they mediate, and vice versa, and see what ruptures, unknowns, contradictions and affiliations can be found and developed. With a speculative approach, there's no need to define binaries, even in order to overcome them or integrate a devalued pole into a valued one (such as art and labour, art and life, art and politics, etc.). Instead we constantly redefine our terms through the kinds of questions the artwork asks, and asks of us. We can then see the divisions we encounter as themselves historical, needing to be explained rather than described, and explained often in terms of systemic as well as local social contradiction and specificity. Thus speculation, both as method and as a field of study and praxis, necessitates a situated perspective, but also a readiness for that perspective to shift, both in light of its objects and the changing problematics and imperatives of knowledge production in its social, historical and economic relations and antagonisms. In this way, the 'speculative' is brought into contact with the 'materialist', with the former the vector of transformation and the latter of social reality. As tendencies, as constitutive of relations rather than objects, and objects as temporary crystals of relations in a wider 'social synthesis', these comprise the touchstones for my work as a whole.

With all this in mind, it may yet be necessary to add two more granular reservations. Given the speculative infrastructure of contemporary capitalism, apparently science-adjacent 'research-based' and 'fictioning' or narrative approaches to art practice

13 G. W. F. Hegel, *The Science of Logic*, translated by George di Giovanni, Cambridge: Cambridge University Press, 2010; Denise Ferreira da Silva, 'Difference Without Separability' (2008), are.na.

are themselves determined by speculative capitalism, which shapes its market, institutional structure and forms of data. A documentary or 'forensic' aesthetic is no more, or less, integrated into the speculative than a more material-, object- or fantasy-based one. It is not the content of the art but how labour is exchanged, distributed and represented that counts – that is, how it is inscribed into circuits of valorisation even when it is not directly 'value-producing' in itself. By the same token, 'infrastructure' or the 'infrastructural' should not be reduced to the gestural emphasis placed by more or less progressive art institutions on those aspects of their mission statements that speak to a 'usefulness' for the production, display and contextualisation of art.[14] This would be within the understanding of the institution as a neutral enabler of culture, a notion that aligns, unsurprisingly, with the customer-facing neutrality structurally embraced, if performatively denied, by all large profit-making entities. Rather, infrastructural critique needs to deepen the critique of the institution of art by approaching its conditions *as an infrastructure* and speculatively turning these to new ends. An organisational rather than thematic appropriation of the labour in art, I would argue, is the only way that a negative critique of autonomy can be initiated by using the institutional and infrastructural resources of that autonomy, allowing it to transversally connect with and through movements elsewhere, and to materialise those movements within the space of art as a concrete rather than gestural politics. At a theoretical level, we could frame the key critical question by transposing Marx's question about labour to art: the point is not to find the value *behind* the social form of art, but to ask, instead, why is it that, in our society, value often takes the form of art? At a practical

14 Larne Abse Gogarty, '"Usefulness" in Contemporary Art and Politics', *Third Text*, 31, 1: 1–16.

level, we might think of Vilém Flusser's concept of 'envisioning', which Flusser defines as 'trying to turn an automatic apparatus against its own condition of being automatic'.[15]

Over the past few years, throughout the particular crises that have dominated our lives and awareness – episodes of climate collapse by fire and water, the pandemic and the horrific military campaigns attacking the people of Syria, Palestine, Yemen and Ukraine – we have also heard a lot about what is often called 'critical infrastructures', that is, the power grid, server architecture/internet, water supplies, all the semi-automated networks key to our survival that a depletion of supplies, a system fault or a malicious hacking operation can render dysfunctional, with destructive as well as unpredictable consequences that themselves depend on how long such systems remain 'off-line'. These scenarios of destruction have, of course, already taken place, wherever there has been a climate-crisis-induced natural disaster such as flooding and fire, or as a consequence of war. This notion of critical infrastructure, and the resources and workers that keep it operating or are vulnerable to attack, are central to my understanding of critique as such. The point is to show how the category of critique changes when it is posited on an infrastructural and not simply discursive level – when it ceases to be an implicit language of institutional accountability – as well as to see how the operation of critique can generate new relations between distinct discursive and infrastructural levels. But as usual we also need to turn the question around, to ask whether the discursive and philosophical notion of critique, which has been justifiably queried from so many perspectives over the recent period, can itself be a 'critical infrastructure' for how organisational and political change

15 Vilém Flusser, *Into the Universe of Technical Images*, translated by Nancy Ann Roth, Minneapolis: Minnesota University Press, 2011, 19.

happens in the space of art, where critique is so often treated as the property of a Eurocentric 'modernism'.

Infrastructures of race

Infrastructure persists and makes possible only insofar as it also makes *impossible.* At this point, we can align a thinking of infrastructure as conditions of reproduction with Michel Foucault's discussion of regimes of governmentality, the purpose of which is to make live and let die.[16] Infrastructure is always specific: it is sustained and maintained to achieve certain biopolitical outcomes, to enable certain strategies of accumulation that are founded on destroyed environments for many, insofar as it supports accumulation for some. In other words, it is premised on the extraction and waste disposal of labours, lives and natures; as Zandi Sherman argues in her article 'Infrastructures and the Ontological Question of Race', race is itself an infrastructure that mediates access to resources, the withholding of which is key to the population management on which efficient extraction of wealth is premised.[17]

Such differentiated management of 'infrastructural coercion' and 'infrastructural neglect' recalls Ruth Wilson Gilmore's key formulation of racism as 'the state-sanctioned [. . .] group-differentiated vulnerability to premature death'.[18] Death by infrastructure, as in large areas inhabited by communities subject to

16 Michel Foucault, 'Truth and Power', in *Power/Knowledge: Selected Interviews and other Writings 1972–77*, translated by Colin Gordon et al., New York: Pantheon Books, 1980, 121.

17 Zandi Sherman, 'Infrastructures and the Ontological Question of Race', *e-flux*, September 2021, e-flux.com.

18 Ruth Wilson Gilmore, *Golden Gulag: Prisons, Surplus, Crisis, and Opposition in Globalizing California*, Berkeley: University of California Press, 2007, 28.

environmental racism, unfolds in the shadows of death by police violence, death by poverty and deaths of despair; it could arguably even be said to serve as a precondition for all of these. And yet, if infrastructure should be identified and historicised as the material basis for violent processes of racialisation, for a materialist analysis it is crucial as well to look at the other side of this argument. Who benefits? Notably, extractive corporations and the perma-colonial states in which they are imbricated, now reproduced at a global scale. For Sherman, infrastructural and ontological lenses are not opposed: 'infrastructure is ontological', because it is the material basis for the reproduction of race. The social being of race is produced by the operations of extractive infrastructure, and race is an infrastructure in its own right, a condition of reproduction, legitimating the normalised violence that physical infrastructure both captures and extends.

If we stick to the idea that race is an infrastructure, what else does it make possible, as the converse of its pedagogy of abjection and disavowal? As thinkers such as Sylvia Wynter, David Lloyd and Denise Ferreira da Silva have elaborated, what it makes possible is the Western bourgeois 'conception of the human, Man, which overrepresents itself as if it were the human itself'.[19] As Lloyd shows in relation to the homologous foundation of modern aesthetics and politics, Man as the overdetermined human takes centre stage as the rational subject who creates and maintains infrastructures of progress and abundance where once there was only subsistence and warfare.[20] The human is figured as the bringer of infrastructure to a chaotic nature, with infrastructure

19 Sylvia Wynter, 'Unsettling the Coloniality of Being/Power/Truth/Freedom: Towards the Human, After Man, Its Overrepresentation – An Argument', *CR: The New Centennial Review*, 3, 3 (2003): 260.

20 David Lloyd, *Under Representation: The Racial Regime of Aesthetics*, New York: Fordham University Press, 2018.

and property claims coming to light at the same moment. As English-language predicates such as 'humane' and concepts such as humanity and humanism demonstrate, the human marks the point of inextricability of domination and care which an infrastructure can be said to materialise – a coherent moral subject that 'lives off ... the expropriation of the total value produced by native lands and slave labor'.[21]

So can we jettison this figure of normativity while holding on to a notion of ethics, such as the 'poethics' of existence without the 'separability' that social domination introduces? Arguably, this invalidates the assumption that politics requires a normative reference of some kind, in order to ground its claim to the necessity and desirability of transformation. My own sense is that we need to frame the levels of entanglement between the ethical approach and social antagonism through the category of the negative. The pragmatic negativity of infrastructural critique could serve this purpose, perhaps, recognising that, insofar as we are situated in a space of 'operations', it is a contradictory one, optimised for the valorisation of capitalist time and favouring the extraction of the resources that guarantee it.[22] Infrastructure can be conceived in these terms as a kind of 'second nature' – a product of human activity treated *as if* it were something natural – that can be collectively transformed for different ends, because it was collectively made and is the enabling condition for anything we

21 Denise Ferreira da Silva, 'Toward a Black Feminist Poethics. The Quest(ion) of Blackness Toward the End of the World', *TBS*, 44, 2 (2014), 97.

22 Mezzadra and Neilson, *The Politics of Operations: Excavating Contemporary Capitalism*, Durham: Duke University Press, 2019: 'We ... steer clear of understanding extraction, logistics, and finance merely as economic sectors ... Instead, we treat extraction, logistics, and finance as intersecting sets of operations and practices' (4).

can do and think.[23] This argument opens out onto the complex problem of *reproduction*, familiar from the history of feminist debates about maintenance and care; a term fraught with ethical imperatives that we will discuss, in relation to feminist art and politics, in Chapter 4. For now, we can say simply that it allows the negativity of infrastructural critique to adopt the standpoint of transformation, since the infrastructure is both the basis for miserable and distorted life and the resource for very different types of coordination, along with the subjectivities that would struggle to realise them.

Bridge as de facto wall

With the foregoing consideration of critical praxis, what has been elided so far are the many debates around blockage, occupation and sabotage and their efficiency in disrupting a capitalism wholly dependent on the functionality of supply chains, on the just-in-time circulation of objects, services and data along waterways, pipelines, fibreoptic cables and transport systems. This kind of practical critique of infrastructure has been extensively theorised in recent discussions, whether it is in terms of struggles that include dimensions of decolonial and indigenous sovereignty, such as the multiple pipeline-blocking movements in North America since 2018's NoDAPL, or the blockage of West Coast ports in the United States. Aside from the agency of organised pushback, of course, there are the ongoing significant logistical drags – particularly visible during the years of the Covid-19 pandemic – such as labour shortages, high fuel prices and

23 For 'second nature' see Christoph Menke, 'Hegel's Theory of Second Nature', *Symposium: Canadian Journal of Continental Philosophy/Revue canadienne de philosophie continentale*, 17, 1 (2013).

back-ups in shipping lanes. More generally, theorists such as Joshua Clover contended in the mid-2010s that sabotage has gained an epochal salience in an era when capitalism's secular tendency to flee from production into circulation (covering sectors from transport to services to financialisation) has meant not just that it is more vulnerable to forms of logistical sabotage, but that sabotage, blockage and riot are the dominant modes of antagonism.[24]

Blockage also becomes a way of thinking art production or art institutions that orient themselves towards the 'infrastructure'. In this sense, it is clear that infrastructural *critique* has made inroads here, though it remains a minoritarian tendency when measured against the pervasiveness of representational and narrative strategies. We can discuss infrastructural critique with reference to movements around labour organising in arts institutions, such as the wave of unionising of art workers since the beginning of the pandemic, as well as social movements focusing on arts institutions that centre anti-colonial solidarity at arts institutions, such as Decolonize This Place or Strike MoMA in NYC, to take two important movements of the 2010s and early 2020s.[25] Once again, the point here has to do with the critique of material conditions of reproduction. These were interventionist projects inhabiting the gap between art institutions' gestural benevolence and material violence, and prioritising radical disruption as a form of solidarity with struggles elsewhere, predominantly around police violence, racialised gentrification or the colonial war against Palestinians. Yet, within our framework, infrastructural critique can also characterise specific practices of artists and institutions, as a move that similarly takes

24 Joshua Clover, *Riot, Strike, Riot: The New Era of Uprisings*, London: Verso, 2016.

25 For Decolonize This Place, see decolonizethisplace.org; for Strike MoMA, see its entry on Wikipedia.

their practice beyond the comfort zone of reflexivity and thus veers away from the 'lane' allocated to it by institutional critique.

These practices raise instructive questions about what types of infrastructure an art practice might seek to block. In Cameron Rowland's intensively researched and conceptually adroit projects, the central focus is the apparatus of racialised capitalism as a spectrum of real abstractions. These real abstractions, or abstractions with deadly effects, include race, property and value, as they work through prisons, police and cultural and state authorities, now and in the abiding past. These abstractions in turn provide both formal and practical tools for an aesthetics that is not so much documentarian or forensic as it is prismatic. On the point of involving the arts institution in a financial market venture, there is an echo of early institution-critical projects such as Robert Morris's *Money* (1969), in which the artist arranged a series of financial transactions between museum, collector and himself and then exhibited the corresponding legal documentation as the 'materials' of the work. The difference is in the politics and the purpose: it is not about disclosing something now evident about the art institution's intimacy with speculative capital. Such an intimacy is only one symptom among many of the ties between culture and private property, with dispossession as the basis of both. There is often a pedagogical performativity involved, which both presents a detailed historical array of texts and a selective summoning of artefacts at the same time as a real-time deployment of that same legal machinery that upholds the sanctity of property, present and past. A partial list would be 2020's *Encumbrance* at London's ICA, which involved the mortgaging of the royal building's mahogany fittings, obtained in colonial trade; 2017's *Public Money*, which required the Whitney to invest in anti-recidivism social impact bonds issued by a California municipality; *Disgorgement* (2016), the establishment of an insurance trust held in the name of Artists Space (since collected by MoMA), which bought shares in the slave insurance policies still

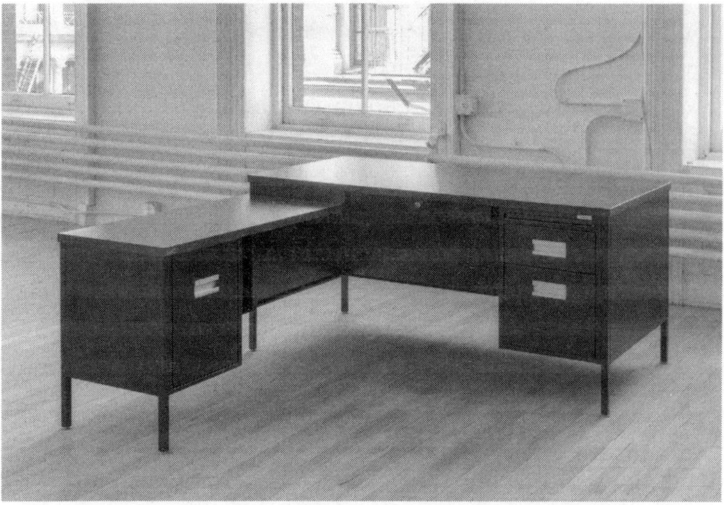

Cameron Rowland, *Attica Series Desk*, 2016. Steel, powder coating, laminated particleboard, distributed by Corcraft. 60 × 71.5 × 28.75 inches. Rental at cost.

Artwork text: *The Attica Series Desk is manufactured by prisoners in Attica Correctional Facility. Prisoners seized control of the D-Yard in Attica from 9 to 13 September 1971. Following the inmates' immediate demands for amnesty, the first in their list of practical proposals was to extend the enforcement of 'the New York State minimum wage law to prison industries'. Inmates working in New York State prisons are currently paid $0.10 to $1.14 an hour. Inmates in Attica produce furniture for government offices throughout the state. This component of government administration depends on inmate labor.*

Artworks indicated as 'Rental at cost' are not sold. Each of these artworks may be rented for five years for the total cost of the Corcraft products that constitute it.

held by a major global insurer, and which will pay out in the event of federal financial reparations for chattel slavery in the US; and *91020000* (2016), which put on display the mobile infrastructure of the public realm in the state of New York – school and office furniture made by prison labour (see photo above). Many of these objects cannot be sold to any collection but only rented, at cost – that is, the price paid at a police auction or to a prison-made furniture manufacturer – for a period of five years pending renewal or return to the artist. In much of Rowland's work, a piece of infrastructure relates a history of property and dehumanisation through the way it functions, rather than in what it uses artistic means to depict. This, in conjunction with the frequent implication of the institution as a 'collaborator' (both with Rowland and the system they are highlighting), is one move that establishes their project as infrastructural rather than institutional critique.

In an essay by the artist and Distributed Cognition Cooperative member Anna Engelhard, contextualising her project *The Crimean Bridge*, she contends that the politics of infrastructure are often cloaked by the image of utility, which, in the case of a bridge, assumes the even more benign trappings of connection, as opposed to the conflict signalled by a wall.[26] This dovetails with the geographer Timothy Mitchell's argument that infrastructure should be thought in terms of how its self-evident performativity (whether efficient or degraded) 'imped[es] us from thinking differently'.[27] Performativity, in Mitchell's approach, delineates a discursive and a functional layer to how we relate to infrastructure as an everyday part of the landscape. For him, capitalist valorisation is predicated

26 Anna Engelhardt, 'Adversarial Infrastructure: The Crimean Bridge', *Mute*, 7 July 2020, metamute.org.

27 Timothy Mitchell, 'Infrastructures Work on Time', *e-flux*, January 2020, e-flux.com.

on the possibility of delay – of capturing the future in the present, which is to say, of *extracting* from the future to substantiate value claims and preserve assets in the present, leaving very little future for those who might want to organise it differently. The bridge constructed by Russia over the Kerch Strait between Russia and the Crimean Peninsula is analysed by Engelhardt as an impediment in quite literal terms, as a disguised 'wall' or border, facilitating Russian economic colonialism in Ukraine before, during and after its 2014 annexation. This is a model of infrastructure as 'war by other means', which might also characterise social media platforms such as Facebook, depicted as global engines of connection even as they facilitate multi-scalar conflict – a trope familiar from eighteenth-century ideologists of capitalism who juxtaposed civilised commerce to war, blithely averting the gaze from the inseparability between them established by several centuries of settler colonialism and trade in humans that had already elapsed by the time those texts were written.

Working with this example of logistics that communicates flow even while enforcing restriction and promoting repression in the guise of mobility, Engelhardt disassembles the bridge in her essay while the eponymous film uses volumetrics, crystallography, clips of RT reports and other technical media to reassemble it in all its dimensions as a species of 'hybrid warfare' with ecological and geopolitical impacts that unfold over several temporalities. Here, the infrastructural critique does not show the recursive volatility that comes from implicating its own material sites of enunciation as part of the object, as with Cameron Rowland's work. However, the site of enunciation may get another spin here – it is not the art institution that is key, but digital platforms. It is the media-propaganda complex as an instrument of reproduction that is at stake in this work, combining advanced technology and crude manipulation, the logistics of war and the logistics of trade. Infrastructure figures in Engelhardt's work as the real abstraction of communication that is at the core of violence, with property just one of its symptoms.[28]

Finally, and in a change of key, it may be helpful to take a preliminary look at an instance of organisational rather than artistic practice, in which *learning* from artistic practice is the principal strategy. An example here is the exhibition *Reconsidering Institutional Conduct (Almost Everything Still Remains to be Done)*, curated by Eric Golo Stone at Künstlerhaus Stuttgart in 2021, which invited the artists and cultural workers Heba Y. Amin, Grayson Earle, Irena Haiduk, Clara Sukyoung Jo, Sandrine Micossé-Aikins, Anike Joyce Sadiq, Anna Schiefer, Bea Schlingelhoff, Ülkü Süngün and Stefan Wäldele to prepare a code of conduct for the institution itself. The project's relation to infrastructural critique could be detected precisely in the 'inward- and outward-facing' task it set itself, to revisit its protocols of institutional governance as a site of radical remaking in a wider social landscape that desperately required revolutionary change, and which could start with where it was as a site of implementation of that change, part of which meant rethinking the boundaries of the Künstlerhaus's own inside and outside.

The Künstlerhaus Stuttgart joins a number of 'drafting' projects situated in arts institutions over the past decade. A network of smaller and medium-size contemporary art institutions have participated in or facilitated this institutional shift, exemplified by the drafting of a 'Convention on the Use of Space' organised by Adelita Husni-Bey with local housing groups in 2018, as well as the initiation of a 'Climate Justice Code' for arts organisations in 2019, both at Casco (now the

28 Marina Vishmidt, 'Speculation in a Sense: Aesthetics and Real Abstraction', in *In the Mind but Not from There*, edited by Gean Moreno, London: Verso, 2019.

Casco Art Institute – Working for the Commons) in Utrecht.[29] This suggests that, at least for a fraction of smaller Western arts organisations, a self-perception of themselves as infrastructure – as a part of the functional social landscape – is starting to supplant a traditional concept of the institution as a detached container that displays aspects of that landscape. The repercussions of this type of shift may be variable and intermittent, as well as local, in both the geographic but also the discursive senses of the term. The histories of DIY cultures invoked earlier suggest both the strengths and the weaknesses of this approach. No doubt, there are risks of insularity if the drive for reflexivity leads to an over-emphasis on the agency of the institution rather than its conditions of possibility. While this is connected to, if not determined by, broader levels of social struggle, it is also influenced by the vision of political agency an arts institution chooses to embody and/or amplify in its own situation.

A huge hovering bear

At a fundamental level, infrastructural critique begins from the assumption that it is possible to completely sidestep all the handwringing over the limits of the institution and instead acknowledge what resources are there, how they can be repurposed, which ones cannot and which ones are needed. As my comments on *Reconsidering Institutional Conduct (Almost Everything Still Remains to Be Done)* suggest, the whole

29 In 2013, Casco decided to take the step of reconceiving of its institutional infrastructure as a 'commons', a process described by its director Binna Choi in a conversation for the 'I Is for Institute' project, see iisforinstitute.icaphila.org.

premise of infrastructural critique is to forget about insides and outsides as limits or borders for us – which is what 1980s and 1990s institutional critique often boiled down to, until its austerity was upgraded and franchised by relational aesthetics – and take them up as part of the productive equipment afforded to us by the art field, both economically and ideologically.[30] The attempt to leave behind the boundedness of the institution is, in turn, related to an ambivalence I have always felt towards sectarianism of all kinds, in leftist and communist as well as art-field politics: the search for radical coherence, a position-taking that is not so much an escape from a feeling of marginality as a direct expression of it, though it often takes a displaced form. What does this book provide instead? A non-deterministic approach to social antagonism, especially from the viewpoint of practice. Alongside that, a commitment to taking the speculative subject, the self-optimising doom of creativity, ingrained in artistic subjectivation, as well as the confidence in experimentation that an artistic education can impart, and turning these inside out as resources for experimental forms of connecting and infrastructures of organising. The first section of the book will lay out the fundamental categories and timelines required for an approach to infrastructural critique, while the second will set out a series of categories or 'prismatic drills' through which to conceive a speculative politics within the infrastructure. This is, I argue, one way of thinking speculation and infrastructure alongside one another: what I propose is that the 'means of abstraction' or speculation also need to be thought from the bottom up and inside out, in conjunction with social struggle, and the question of abstraction is not just about control but also can give

30 For further discussion on the Kantian history of boundary setting, see Vishmidt, 'Hard Labour of Speculation', 1.

us a relational view on artistic and economic practices as they constitute social *forms*: the smallest meaningful unit of a politically entangled art-historical, art-theoretical method.

Where this takes us will be examined in the following chapters, but maybe a final touchstone for now is Jeff VanderMeer's novel *Borne*, with its huge hovering bear that terrorises everyone in a town but then its fur becomes a rich repository for scavengers when it's asleep. The allegory can accompany us as we try to think the relation of institutional to infrastructural critique and of critique to antagonism as the boundary between inside and out breaks down – insofar as it can be said to have existed in the first place.

2.

Critique, Institutional and Infrastructural

Shifts and drifts

There has always been a resonant paradox at the heart of institutional critique, one that can be framed in Kantian terms: as institutional critique works to expose its transcendental conditions – the contradictions of the institution of art – it amplifies rather than undermines them. If Western art institutions can be seen as plenipotentiaries of a contested – or embattled – Enlightenment legacy (depending on how you look at it), then the artistic strategy of institutional critique was fated from the start to slot into the master's toolbox, however fervently it has been avowed to be the most serious, if not the only, political implement that artists have at their disposal.[1] As with Kant's project, it has aimed to clarify the legitimate bounds of critique. The bounds have been drawn around the type of critique artists could level at the institution of art, while also embodying it professionally, socially, psychologically and economically – that is, to stake out a position of good and bad faith simultaneously, the classic double bind. This soldered artists and institutions together in an increasingly half-hearted *tableau vivant* of autonomy, a reconciled realpolitik not all that different from the kind that anointed liberal democracy as the least-worst form of government still standing after everything else had ostensibly been tried.

1 Andrea Fraser, 'From the Critical Institutions to an Institution of Critique,' *Artforum*, 44, 1 (September 2005), 278–83.

If this schema appears somewhat on the reductive side, that may be because the libidinal economy of institutional critique has had a number of other facets. Kafka's 'A Report to an Academy' evokes that aspect of institutional critique that entails dressing up in the master's clothes as an affront to the master's society.[2] The mode here would owe less to constructive criticism and more to the apotropaic vaudeville of Jean Rouch's *Les maîtres fous* (1955), with its plebeian cultists acting out the spirits of French colonial administration. Here we could think about the address of such modes of critique to institutions which have traversed but are not contained by the institution of art – institutions such as white supremacy, patriarchy, capitalism – and how the art institution could be repurposed to put these institutionalised exclusions on view, if not redress them. Such an expanded notion of 'institution' would reflect the expansive, sociologically and psychoanalytically inflected sense of 'institution' deployed by, for example, Andrea Fraser. We can employ this widened definition of institutional critique here retrospectively to analyse the relationships between activist practices in and out of the 'art world' in the period the term usually encompasses: from the late 1960s to the early 1990s.

Troubling the historical parameters of 'first-' and 'second-generation' institutional critique, with its solidified division into an era that emphasised fixed (Michael Asher) or variable capital (Fraser), we find collective and individual practices sometimes in alliance with campaigns led by organisations such as the Women's Liberation Art Group, the Art Workers' Coalition or the American Indian Movement – artists Adrian Piper, Jimmie Durham, David Hammons, the Guerrilla Girls, VALIE EXPORT, William Pope.L, to take a more or less haphazard sample. The radicalisations and

2 Franz Kafka, 'A Report to an Academy', in *Franz Kafka: The Complete Stories*, edited by Nahum N. Glazer, New York: Shocken Books, 1983, 250–63.

individuations enacted in these historical instances may surface in the work of more recent generations of artists, if often manneristically. But their key significance was in laying a track between the critique of institutions and the critique of infrastructures – that is, not simply the formal but the material conditions that located the institution in an expanded field (of structural violence). The 'extra-murality' of this tendency was taken up later as a call to build, or at least model, institutions, whether in the temporary sociality of the project, the erratic durability of the project space or the ambient resource economies of the research cluster, the more recent history of which we touched on at the end of the last chapter. The question of what would thereby constitute the 'formal' and the 'material' could perhaps be displaced to consider rather the matter of whether these institution-critical practices situated themselves principally in an 'immanent' or a 'transversal' relation to the spaces of artistic exhibition and discourse. The materiality of the art institution would, for example, form the centre of Asher's excavation projects,[3] and the disturbance of its architectural layers would be a means of exposing other social and symbolic parameters of its existence – yet it would be the physical fabric that stayed at the core of these implications. A similar framing would apply to Fraser, for whom the protocols and economies of the mainstream field of art would be the substance and the subject of critique, with the wider social conditions for its existence as backdrop to be disclosed by implication. The Art Workers' Coalition could be considered as mediating the

3 One of the oft-cited examples would be the intervention at Galleria Toselli in Milan in 1973, when Asher sandblasted many years of layers of white paint off the wall, reuniting the brick with the concrete of the floor. Asher wrote that 'the withdrawal of the white paint, in this case, became the objectification of the work'. See Anne Rorimer, 'Context as Content', *Texte zur Kunst*, 1 (Autumn 1990).

immanent and the transversal with its campaigns addressing systemic social inequality in the representational spaces of art.[4] The present-day group We Are Here, on the other hand, could be seen as more transversal insofar as the institution of art is deployed as an occasional platform for a systemic critique of border regimes and white supremacy as functional institutions reproducing European society via the normalised coercion of exclusion.[5] However, the formal/material, immanent/transversal filter should not signify a desire to perpetuate dualities that divide trained artists from activist groups, especially if both are viewed as 'users' of art institutions. Rather, the question is where the institution of art is situated within different practical approaches to institutional critique – is it exemplary but contingent, or is it a principal focus, treated as the only valid site of dissidence for those who would inscribe their activities in the space of art? In trying to develop a longer-term perspective on the theoretical arguments of the previous chapter, I argue here that the difference is not always clear, but that it is the former tendency (or focus) that allows us to more clearly track a shift – perhaps, rather, a *drift* – from an institutional to an infrastructural critique. As already outlined, 'infrastructure', like 'institution', is used in a rather flexible way, but

4 The Art Workers' Coalition formed in New York in 1969 with a list of demands presented to the Museum of Modern Art. See Lucy Lippard, 'The Art Workers' Coalition: Not a History', in *Get the Message? A Decade of Art for Social Change*, New York: E. P. Dutton, 1984, 10–20.

5 We Are Here is an organisation of refugees who have united in Amsterdam to bring their collective struggle in the Netherlands into public discussion. Consisting of 225 immigrants from approximately fifteen countries, their search for asylum has failed, and yet for a variety of reasons they cannot be sent back to their countries of origin. See E. C. Feiss, 'The Art of Resource Development: Here to Support in the Institution of Art', *OAR: The Oxford Artistic and Practice Based Research Platform*, 4 (2021), oarplatform.com.

chiefly to signal a view of the art institution as a site of resources – material and symbolic – and I say drift rather than shift because the development is not clearcut but merely becomes more obvious over time, in the wake of the exhaustion of other strategies. In this light, the construction of institutions may be, at the same time, a practice of institutional *and* infrastructural critique, depending on whether the institution is mainly intended to critically reassess or renew working conditions and visibility in the space of art, or has other ambitions.

In developing this heuristic periodisation, we can perhaps open with the late 1990s and early 2000s, and the development of critical discourses in sociology and politics around the 'project' and 'precarity' as cardinal terms of the deregulated work patterns and cultural milieu of educated, self-motivated strata. Endowed with a readymade unity by neo-Marxian argot such as 'creative class', the 'cognitariat' or, more dystopically, the 'precariat', this was, in reality, a declassed group with eclectic skill-sets whose forms of life often reflected a historically novel (at least in western Europe and North America) middle-class experience of the poorly waged and unstable conditions that had usually been the preserve of the working classes, especially its feminised and racialised segments. Diagnosed by sociologists Luc Boltanski and Eve Chiapello as the children of a bohemian dissidence more interested in individual rebellion than social transformation (which the authors called 'artistic critique')[6] and apostrophised by art critic and activist Brian Holmes as bearers of the 'flexible personality',[7] this was a community that sustained the contradictions of a 'double freedom'[8]

6 Luc Boltanski and Eve Chiapello, *The New Spirit of Capitalism*, translated by Gregory Elliott, London: Verso, 2005.

7 Brian Holmes, 'The Flexible Personality: For a New Cultural Critique', *transversal* (2002), eipcp.net.

8 Marx defined double freedom as the historically unprecedented

rendered more poignant by the horizon of creative self-expression and independent cultural dynamics that drove it forwards. Everywhere could be observed the formation of bohemias dependent on still relatively affordable property prices and still relatively functional social safety nets, not to mention significantly lower personal debt burdens than those that obtain today. Berlin was still Berlin then (if already steeped in Wall-era nostalgia), but so were Munich, Cologne, Zürich ... These were all sites where the early 1990s had seen institutional critique folded into the 'non-productive attitude' (Josef Strau)[9] – the cultivation of persona and community over professional ambition. Approximately a decade later, however, small-time entrepreneurship was overtly on the agenda, and the contradictions of artistic autonomy were emerging with ruthless clarity. The maintenance of free-form community space and centres of autonomous social life as moments of infrastructural critique was vying with the more mimetic forms native to institutional critique, which adapted but also reproduced models of enterprise closer to market and state, such as the gallery, club, boutique and nuclear family. Nonetheless, compared to the austere strictures of the present, the field still seemed relatively open both for experiment and indictment, a phase when the occupation of institutional platforms still seemed to have critical traction. Or it did for transversal art-activist projects – Stephan Dillemuth's, for example – with a looser commitment to finding or making critical space in the

condition of the waged worker in capitalism – the freedom from customary ties (free to sell his or her labour, in other words) and free of means of production (free to starve). For a related proposition in Kant, framed in terms of 'creative labor', see Vishmidt, *Speculation as a Mode of Production*, 183.

9 See Josef Strau, 'The Non-productive Attitude,' in *Make Your Own Life: Artists In and Out of Cologne*, edited by Bennett Simpson, Philadelphia: Institute of Contemporary Art, University of Pennsylvania, 2006, online at s3.amazonaws.com.

institution of art, identifying more with the pedagogy and conviviality of subcultures. This allowed them to avoid the always-incipient academicism of an institutional critique that had, by the late 1990s (or, to listen to its critical supporters, from the very beginning), threatened to become a mode of regulation for the institution – in parallel, perhaps, with the integration of DIY cultures and the obsolescence of the paradigm of 'selling out'.[10]

A small post-Fordist drama

One figure engaged in the kind of critique-by-doing discussed earlier was the artist, educator, writer, curator and researcher Marion von Osten. A perennial engagement with, as well as a tactical emulation of, the tropes of contingency and flexibility as the hallmarks of present-day labour forms one pole of her activity, while the other applies these same categories to national borders and coloniality-laden historicisms such as 'modernity'. From the workers'-inquiry-without-a-workplace scenarios of the group kleines post-fordistisches Drama (kpD, 2004–6), whose film *Kamera läuft!* reconstructed the responses of precarious cultural workers to questions drawn from militant workers' questionnaires produced in Italy in the 1960s (see image below), to the investigations into human and financial fluxes in *MoneyNations* (1998–2000) and *Transit Migration* (2002–6), or the border-eroding radical journals of colonial modernism showcased in *Action! painting/publishing* (2011–12), von Osten's gamut of activity both put into play and thematised a vocational blurring significant for what is here being developed as 'infrastructural critique'.

10 Isabelle Graw, 'Field Work', *Flash Art*, 23, 155 (November–December 1990), 136–7.

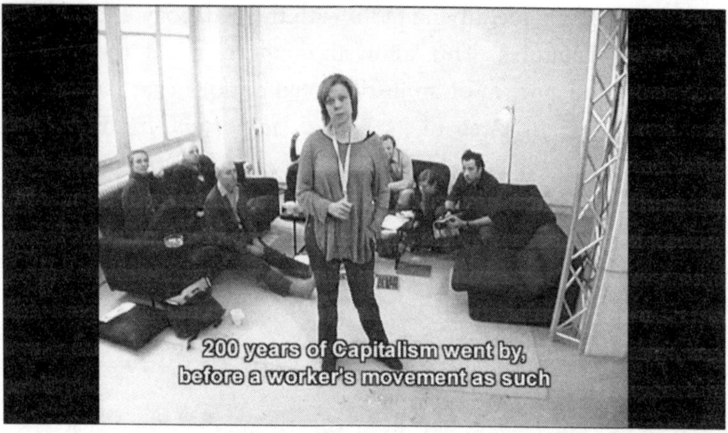

Kleines postfordistisches Drama, *Kamera läuft!*, 2004. Video still of film, by kpD, based on fifteen longer interviews with cultural producers in Berlin using an updated list of questions from militant workers' interviews in Italy in the 1960s.

The phenomenon of transversally minded art-activist practices, which take art institutions as a contingent if motivated site of material resources, started to gain ascendancy from the mid-1990s onwards, coincident with a new rollout of institutional critique pursued from within and on behalf of institutions themselves – the 'New Institutionalism', which sought to index and respond to the diversification and global expansion of the discursive space and markets for art.[11] This now seems like an ephemeral as well as an equivocal moment, whose 'turns' retrospectively seem as driven by imperial as by democratising ambitions, but which also posed one of the last gambits of the bourgeois art institution to refashion itself as a condenser rather than a container of do-it-yourself aspirations

11 Marina Vishmidt, 'The Cultural Logic of Criticality', *Journal of Visual Art Practice*, 7, 3 (2008).

and subcultural alliances.[12] Although this amounts to an unsatisfactory sketch of the broader context for projects like *MoneyNations* or the similarly processual and complex *Ex Argentina* (2002) organised by Alice Creischer and Andreas Siekmann,[13] it supplies enough of a background to highlight what practices of concrete intervention like von Osten's were able to realise here, in the vein of feminist and left-sociological critiques of labour, enunciated from the position of labour.

The domestication of the 'critique of institutions' as the 'institution of critique' has been memorably portrayed by Fraser as a misreading of the original target of institutional critique as anything less than the total social field – with the vital caveat that this is the total social field as it is encapsulated by art.[14] This analysis recast a purported break between an 'objective' (architectural or sociological) institutional critique and the more 'subjective' one of the 1990s (focusing on the gendered and racialised margins of the field and the 'psychic life' of the institutional ego) into a continuity whose watchword was 'total

12 Nina Möntmann, 'The Rise and Fall of New Institutionalism: Perspectives on a Possible Future', in *Art and Contemporary Critical Practice: Reinventing Institutional Critique*, edited by Gerald Raunig and Gene Ray, London: MayFlyBooks, 2009, 155–9; *Art and Its Institutions: Current Conflicts, Critique and Collaborations*, edited by Nina Möntmann, London: Black Dog Publishing, 2006.

13 The project *Ex Argentina* began as an 'economy-critical examination of the economic crisis in Argentina and the international lobbies profiting from it'. See Alice Creischer and Andreas Siekmann, 'Sovereignty of Presence: Real Public Space as Situation', *republicart* (September 2003), republicart.net. These prefigured equally massive and polycentric projects like *The Potosí Principle: How Can We Sing the Song of the Lord in an Alien Land?* (2010–11).

14 Andrea Fraser, 'From the Critique of Institutions to an Institution of Critique', *Artforum*, 44, 1 (September 2005), 278–86.

institution'.[15] The suggestion that this critique could 'ossify' or itself be institutionalised – become, in other words, a defanged 'institution of critique' – was thus deeply misled, according to Fraser, if it suggested that critique could ever be conducted otherwise or elsewhere than fully inside this field.[16] Yet if we consider art as an institution that is far from self-sufficient, relying both on the separation of waged and unwaged 'uncreative' labour and on its constant incorporation materially and symbolically, the imperviousness to an outside seems less than an (enabling) closure for critique and more an alibi for what Denise Ferreira da Silva calls the 'onto-epistemological' closure preserving the 'phantom power' of the art field, inasmuch as it can represent itself to be distinct from the rest of social life, whatever its representational porosity to practices originating far beyond it.[17] When the institution of critique simply (or flatly) becomes coextensive with the institution of art, a Kantian echo chamber of world-historical proportions has truly opened up, possibly designed by architect Frank Gehry. A move to infrastructural critique represents an attempt to mediate some of the closures of this position both discursively and pragmatically, with infrastructure focusing the link between the material and ideological conditions of the institution of art in a way that decentres rather than affirms it.

---

15 Compare to the 'total policing' motto of the London Metropolitan Police: content.met.police.uk. The aims and questionable punctuation of the Met's statement seem hardly dissimilar to those held by many other institutions that do not treat crime-fighting as one of their missions, art institutions included.

16 An interesting contribution to this debate is Suhail Malik's idea of 'anarcho-realism' and related call for 'institutions of negation'. See his series titled 'On the Necessity of Art's Exit from Contemporary Art', Artists Space, May–June 2013, online at artistsspace.org.

17 Denise Ferreira da Silva, 'Notes for a Critique of the "Metaphysics of Race"', *Theory, Culture and Society*, 28, 1 (January 2011): 138–48.

And yet if the institution is purportedly reproduced in every act of artistic authorship, the entanglement in the collective that von Osten has maintained in each of her projects has been a riposte to this condition: an endeavour boosted by the institutional insecurities and robust subcultures of the mid-1990s to early 2000s. The challenge to the sovereignty of the artist, even when activists or collectives take that role, transpires ultimately as a challenge to authorship. This, perhaps, yields some indication of the multivalence of von Osten's practice as curator, arts organiser, writer and artist, activities that were not separated in time or by project but that unfolded simultaneously, in a practical flouting of the division of labour that allows such 'border-crossing' gestures to be authored and thus to register. This is a strategy that amounts not simply to displacing a theoretical or social commodity into an art space, but to re-performing the social relations of non-sovereign art contexts in the institution without claiming authorship in the performance. The art institution then becomes a contingent locale for infrastructural critique that stages or recruits – that siphons – capital from this site of materialisation but does not foreground it, thus damming a reverse flow of critical 'capital' back into the institution.

Another frame should also interest us here. Von Osten's flouting of the division of labour represents a departure from another 'disordering', namely the conventional avant-garde precept that the politics of art depends on the 'derangement of the senses'. Her deliberately contingent occupation of the institution of art – in all its infra-thin dimensions – signalled a sidestepping of this political claim, one whose valorisation of derangement often reproduced, under the guise of overturning, the normative containers of the aesthetic. As in Pilvi Takala's somewhat later work *The Trainee* (2008), in which the artist spent an internship at a financial services company visibly doing 'brain work', aka nothing, von Osten's projects, such as the knowingly titled group kpD or *Atelier Europa*, made labour visible where it should be invisible (in the space of art) by displacing the protocols of its inclusion in that space (as found object, as scandal) and, instead, focusing on the conditions of production of the artwork as the immediately social ones of cooperative (if fragmented) labour. As projects dwelling in the then not-yet customary zone of indistinction between the curatorial, the artistic and academic research, they were proleptically *indisciplinary* in a way that could be interpreted as either 'too' elusive or 'too' fitting in the era of 'New Institutionalism': their clarity of purpose and complexity of orchestration could only have come into focus through the rearview. In other words, it is the retrospection afforded by the stabilisation of 'social engagement' as a genre, on the one hand, and the spectacular staging of the social in the social media-fed works of, for example, Ryan Trecartin, on the other, that lend the previously described projects precision and tentativeness at the same time – something the horizon of the 2010s and 2020s may have become too congested and cynical to support. The connection to the 'outside' that the projects have, to the sociality and work routines that traverse and exceed the exhibition space – however it is configured or displaced – steps back from making political claims as appended to this act of appearance and thus drains the institution of critique of its heady fragrance. At the same time, the precarity, porosity and opportunism of this near-beyond can also be seen in sharp relief: a bohemianism of evasion instead of an emphatic solidarity of condition. Something rather loose, disparate, pedantic and effortful can be detected instead. This mode of engagement, in many ways superseded by the forms of infrastructural critique discussed in the chapters to follow, nevertheless suggests a form of self-directed obstinacy we can recognise from Oskar Negt and Alexander Kluge:

> A daring hypothesis emerges that partially flies in the face of the bulk of historical empiricism: all this points to the core

> of labour power's self-will. The need for the confederation and association of producers (as a subjective labour capacity and labour power) does not objectify itself because of the obstinacy of those needs.[18]

What also seems salient in this paradigm is the visibility of a community of practice. The argument that small, dialogic and reflexive communities could pursue an antagonistic praxis in relation to an ever more autonomised and bureaucratised art world was already being advanced in the mid-1970s as a counter to the gesturality of 'institutional critique', first coined in 1975 by artist Mel Ramsden in his incisive essay 'On Practice' in the first issue of *The Fox*, the journal put out by the New York–based faction of Art and Language:

> To dwell perennially on an institutional critique without addressing specific problems within the institutions is to generalize and sloganize. It may also have the unfortunate consequence of affirming that which you set out to criticize. It may even act as a barrier to eventually setting up a community practice (language ... sociality ...) which does not just embody a commodity mode of existence.[19]

---

18 Stewart Martin, 'Political Economy of Life: Negt and Kluge's *History and Obstinacy*', *Radical Philosophy*, 190 (March–April 2015), 32.

19 Mel Ramsden, 'On Practice', *The Fox*, 1, 1 (1975), 69. The introduction of the term is usually attributed to Benjamin H. D. Buchloh's 1990 essay 'Conceptual Art 1962–1969: From the Aesthetic of Administration to the Critique of Institutions', in *Conceptual Art: A Critical Anthology*, edited by Alexander Alberro and Blake Stimson, Cambridge: MIT Press, 1999, 528. Fraser proposes an alternative provenance in 'From the Critique of Institutions to an Institution of Critique', *Artforum*, 44, 1 (September 2005), 278–85.

While the work of an artist like Cameron Rowland requires a somewhat different lens, the era of production that unfolded for von Osten and her collaborators from roughly the mid-1990s to the mid-2000s can still be cognised as an emergent form of infrastructural critique – infrastructural not because the platform won over the content, but because the distinction between platform and content is, in principle, subject to an inquiry with no pre-emptive terminus. From a present-day vantage, the reflexivity of the research method is fascinatingly tentative as well as obstinate, mobilising theoretical templates and social scenes as 'little dramas' that could eventually travel outwards as refrains and quotidian gestures, never coalescing into a critical legacy or trying to transcend 'the creative imperative' (*Be Creative!*, 2003) with the pathos of distance or artistic aura. The aura is itself built into that imperative as a mystification of the 'double freedom' of the cultural worker as a special kind of individual closer to the limitless potential of capital than the hemmed-in dependencies of labour.

In working to situate certain forms of visibility and collectivity within a transversal paradigm, von Osten also actively worked against the exceptionality and romanticism that the watchword 'precarity' no less than 'creativity' often affirmed, just as did 'immaterial labour' slightly later in the sequence of art-world political feelings. In this sense, we can also appreciate her patient, multiple and stubborn trajectory in terms of reproductive labour, as she has explored in *Irene ist Viele!* (Irene Is Many!, 2009),[20] wherein a discussion of director Helke Sander's 1977 film *Die allseitig reduzierte Persönlichkeit – REDUPERS* (All-Around Reduced Personality – Redupers) allowed her to outline the institution of art as a site of collective struggle, alongside the

20 Marion von Osten, 'Irene ist Viele! Or What We Call "Productive Forces"', *e-flux*, 8 September 2009, e-flux.com.

distributed (self-)workplace and the family, for labour both idealised and rendered disposable by the gender system. Sander's film, in which a single mother in her mid-thirties negotiates the tasks of collective art-making and political intervention while raising a child in pre-unification West Berlin, already recognised that subjectivity is both product and process for a disposable workforce of female freelancers. These days, however, the writing seems to be on the wall for ever-growing segments of the working-age population, condemned to a freedom rapidly moving from double to triple (free of tradition, free of means of re/production, free of a market for one's labour-power).

Precarity precarised

This situation then opens up a discussion of how the charting of an itinerary from the critique of institutions to critical institutions and on to infrastructures of critique – in this case, through the prism of somewhat more than two decades of von Osten's exhibition, collaborative and moving image projects – can account for the drastic shifts precipitated by the global socioeconomic crisis unfolding since 2008. If it seems that we don't hear as much about 'precarity' in critical discourse, especially in the field of art, it might say as much about the normalisation of the circumstances that the term identifies, and the widespread adaptation to them, as it does about the attenuated shelf life of theory trends. A poignant example, though not exactly a successful one (perhaps fittingly), is the 2010 film *Eine flexible Frau* by director Tatjana Turanskyj. Fast forward from the era of the chamber tragedies of post-Fordism: here is a survivor of the era of the companionable (if struggling) Berlin bohème, an unemployed architect and lone parent condemned, by her gender, obstinacy and fondness for drink, to 'drifting' (as the English-language title *The Drifter* has it) outside the bounds of the bourgeois security that has absorbed the majority of her peers. The timeline here could be charted like so: *REDUPERS* → kleines postfordistisches Drama → *Eine flexible Frau*. From a politicised feminist community to a more atomised but genial collective of 'cultural producers', to, finally, a woman left in the cold by a gentrified, heteronormative milieu. The film's downcast tone is occasionally leavened by the appearance of a male, Marxist-feminist tour guide on the fringes of the scene, spouting social reproduction theory on the devaluation of feminised labour while leading bemused groups through parks and waste grounds.

Here, we could evoke perhaps Stefano Harney and Fred Moten's recent writing on the 'logistical', which tracks how the colonial logic of racially coded expropriation is gradually being expanded across space to route around subjectivity and accumulate via the exploitation of quantified units in a social space modulated by financial algorithms, securitised environments and social graphs.[21] The replacement of atomised 'creative' individuals by quantified selves perhaps adds another twist to literary theorist Walter Benjamin's 1930s assessment of fascism as masses encouraged to express themselves in lieu of exercising their rights.[22] It also adds a complication to the 'obstinacy' of labour that refuses imperatives of work as well as expressiveness, as mentioned before. It is difficult to counterpoise 'obstinacy' to creativity as a mode of refusal of work when an agential term such as refusal loses critical purchase, in a phase when subjectivity no longer

21 See Harney and Moten, *The Undercommons*; also *All Incomplete*, Colchester: Minor Compositions, 2021.

22 Walter Benjamin, 'The Work of Art in the Age of its Technological Reproducibility', in *The Work of Art in the Age of Its Technological Reproducibility, and Other Writings on Media*, edited by Michael W. Jennings, Brigid Doherty and Thomas Y. Levin, Cambridge: Harvard University Press, 2008, 41.

plays an important role in the regulation of labour.[23] The turn to a colonial architecture of power in the 'first world' as it transitions towards brutal austerity regimes and financialised population management internally and externally highlights the important turn von Osten herself made in the mid- and late 2000s to examining the scope of built and published modernity in the colonial space, as if making a parallel turn to an elsewhere in time and space wherein subjectivity could still (collectively) act as a radical basis or counterpower.[24]

The toy police

In seeking to pursue the implications of von Osten's practice into the present, it is perhaps worth tarrying with the notion of 'little dramas' that kleines post-fordistisches Drama introduces. In fact, we might even speculate here that it is because artistic realisms – like Western labour movements and their strategies of refusal – have less traction today than they did in the decades after World War II, that contemporary artistic approaches need to take a performatively 'infrastructural' tack, in order not merely to reveal, reflect or educate audiences on 'empirical reality' but to emulate aspects of this reality in ways that unhinge

23 Recently debate has shifted away from the focus on subjectivity central to the post-operaist discourse in order to analyse infrastructures such as logistics, finance and management, as well as 'non-human' ecological dimensions. See, for example, Sandro Mezzadra and Brett Neilson, *The Politics of Operations: Excavating Contemporary Capitalism*, Durham: Duke University Press, 2019.

24 See Serhat Karakayalı and Marion von Osten, 'This Was Tomorrow!: Die koloniale Moderne und ihre blinde Flecken', *transversal* (June 2008), transversal.at; and the corresponding exhibition at the Haus der Kulturen der Welt, *Learning from ... Die koloniale Moderne*.

the omnipresent fatalism rooted in its violence, thus shaping and constructing it instead.

At any rate, an extremely literal instance of this approach can be found in the work of Pilvi Takala, who we saw earlier conducting 'brain work' in the open-plan offices of the immediate post-crisis period. Takala's *Close Watch*, which was presented in the Finnish Pavilion at the 59th Venice Biennale of 2022, marked a progression in her ways of working. While the artist had, in the past, often devised projects that found her testing the boundaries of acceptable behaviour in public/private spaces such as Disneyland or shopping malls, in *Close Watch* (2022) we see her as one of the keepers of 'public order'. But what constitutes such an order and whom do its boundaries enclose? These are some of the initial questions raised by the project, and, as we'll see, their ramifications stretch beyond the context in which they're posed. The distinctiveness of Takala's trajectory as an artist has to do with the way that she 'externalises' institutional critique. Which is to say, art is not the target but the resource base for infiltrating professional scenes such as marketing or gaming, or social codes such as carrying money in an opaque container in public or not touching strangers in co-working spaces.

The fact that it is a resource base rather than an alibi is key, as her status as an artist is never revealed or thematised in these uncanny conducts. For *Close Watch*, as in previous projects, she operates on a 'need to know' basis in which managerial higher-ups get informed about the infiltration, but colleagues do not, in order for the ruse to be effective. A significant difference here, however, is that not only did the colleagues google her a couple of weeks before the projected end date of her deployment, but there was no invitation or commission from the side of the company. Nor was there really a ruse, even. *Close Watch* was self-initiated, and all the requisite training (which does not appear to have been extensive) was completed in order to work as a security guard in one of Finland's largest shopping malls. Of equal significance, perhaps, is that the relationships formed at work were extended by months of conversations and filmed 'Forum Theatre' workshops – that is, workshops using the techniques of Theatre of the Oppressed founder Augusto Boal – that involved Takala and her former colleagues, some of which were represented in the piece at the Biennale and in the accompanying publication.[25] In this sense, the piece offers a determined socialisation of the bemused reflexivity that other works of Takala's were concerned with prompting in the viewer, and only secondarily in the other inhabitants of the coded spaces in which she was moving.

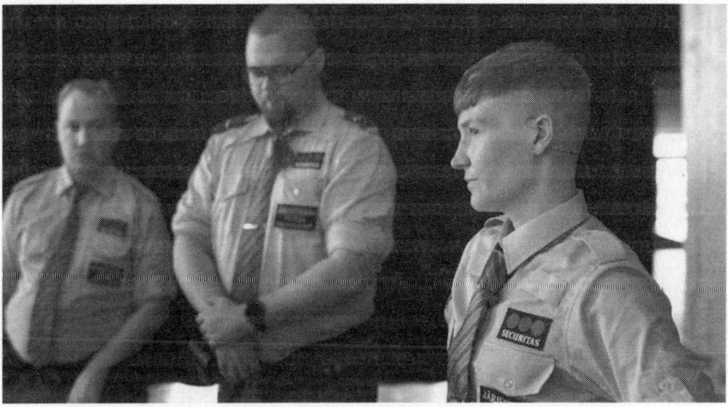

Pilvi Takala, *Close Watch*, 2022. Still of three-channel video installation, 1:08:13, varying dimensions. Photo © Pilvi Takala 2022. Courtesy of the artist; Carlos/Ishikawa, London; and Stigter van Doesburg, Amsterdam.

25 *Pilvi Takala: Close Watch. The Pavilion of Finland – 59th International Art Exhibition, la Biennale di Venezia*, edited by Christina Li, Milan: Mousse Publishing, 2021.

The question of how one is seen is vital here. We could say that, in these scenarios, to be is to appear, and Takala's backstories are sufficiently vague and sufficiently plausible to enable her to appear there, and to function as a reflective element. The genre is often drily comedic, even if the form is documentary. This changes again in the current work. Takala's strong interest in the on-stage and backstage dynamics of discrete professional milieus comes out here in the content – workshop discussions on workplace cultures and how they do or don't influence guard behaviour in public – but also in the form of the work, which is both theatrical and therapeutic, and in the scenography of the installation, which includes a one-way mirror between the videos respectively exploring the 'on' and the 'off' theme. The mid-century North American sociologist Erving Goffman comes to mind here, with his inquiry into everyday behaviour as performative, as it plays to fluid but generally accepted codes of conduct. Notably, *Close Watch*'s scrutiny is not confined to simply querying performativity at work. Its focus is rather on the social and psychic conditions of police violence using the model-train analogy of the security guards as 'toy police', conditions reproduced verbally in the remarks of many of the staff taking part in the workshops, such as when they joke about the security camera as the main disincentive for giving recalcitrant drinkers a good kicking (see still above), or in the first sequence we see, which is a replay of a real-life incident of excessive force that culminated with a knee to the neck. But Takala can also be seen as a Goffmanian comic in her methods, whether she is prompting anxieties in defence of implicit norms or in their literal policing, as is the case here. If her role has generally been to trigger a questioning of codes on the part of those who uphold them by giving them a 'wrong' inflection, then in *Close Watch* that is extended to asking whether the estrangement of norms that such reflexivity is supposed to provoke can itself become a new norm. This sharpened politics of the performative argues that new norms may be needed for a shift away from workplace cultures that reward silence and complicity under the label of 'public order'. But, first, the old ones have to be collectively faced and recognised for what they are.

In watching the videos and reading the conversations with security staff, it's not exactly surprising that gender, race and class shape the working conditions of the 'toy police' just as they do for the 'real' police, with the same issues dominating how they relate to the public. Excess force, manufactured fear, cynicism and the selective solidarity at play in the closing of ranks are all features of the police as an institution. They also appear in the microcosm of Securitas employees, but with even less public oversight. Moreover, with the shopping mall as a privately owned commercial site that is deemed a public space by virtue of its functions (government services as well as stores) under Finnish law, the predicament of the security guards seems to exemplify not only the challenges of public-order policing, but the contradictions of the 'public order' as a core element of the liberal capitalist state: the maintenance of material inequality (order) through formal equality (public). This is a balance that can be struck not only by the silent coercion of the economy but also by the utilisation of controlled force – which Walter Benjamin called the 'law-preserving' violence of the police: the externalisation of anarchy onto a sanctioned social war. It is one half of the proletariat paid to repress the other half, as the mine owners used to boast.

With this brief sketch showing the dilemmas faced by mall security in their generality and particularity, we come back to *Close Watch* as it registers ongoing themes in Takala's work but also pushes them into another space: workplace comedy crosses the line into workplace organising. There is much to be said about the particularity of Takala's methods, which are more infrastructural than conventionally critical in their aims, hoping to transform at least one site or, at best, one corporate culture of a security contractor by 'looking closely' from the inside rather than assembling foregone if correct conclusions from the outside. This inside/outside schema is, of course, inapt, if we stay with the central impulse of all of Takala's adapted Forum Theatre – the outside is just another role on the inside. There is no security guard without a mission to secure public order, and, certainly, there is no public order without a public. The roles are all assigned.

Her participation in this culture as a guard, the guards' participation in the workshop, the methods of Forum Theatre that offer an embodied 'redo' approach to consciousness-raising rather than the simple rehearsal of narratives – all of these suggest that an immanent critique is more effective when it is most performative. Performative not in the sense of doing lip service to a set of emancipatory principles without doing anything more structural to realise them, but in the sense of using performance to step back from, to estrange, the everyday performativity that all labour, including the most functional and most dispiriting types of service work, such as mall security, already requires. Here, Takala's collaboration with Forum Theatre trainers, to help her and her former colleagues unpick the relations and routines between them, underlines that change has to come from the inside, if an inside is suddenly held at arm's length so it can be enacted differently. It also indexes the space between Forum Theatre and the defamiliarisation techniques familiar from Bertolt Brecht and approaches that he influenced. While those methods were geared towards making the familiar strange as part of a collective political project hostile to the pacifying effects of capitalist culture, their digestion by that culture over time means that pacification now equally attends those ways of 'making strange', turning them into a spectacle that no longer repels experience but consumes it (which is the contribution to the efficiency of the culture machine made by platform media). The imperative, then, to catalyse performativity in and against performativity recalls Ray Brassier's point that the 'problem is to convert an experience of estrangement to the estrangement of experience'.[26] It is first an experience of the reorganisation of senses and affects about what is real and what is tolerable, and doesn't all organising have to start there?

From the vantage point of the present, we can see a continuity between von Osten's work and Takala's, such that the former was all along pursuing a specific type of infrastructural critique – kaleidoscopic, sophisticated, transversal, yet also provisional and delaminated from the subjective and critical authority wielded by most artist-as-curator practices. In both cases, labour is the central focus, which perhaps begins to explain why institutional critique is jettisoned in the span of work under examination, and we return to where we began.[27] If the project of critique always ends up affirming its subject – the institution of art – in its valorisation of both the affective subject and its critical capacity, this can inflate the artist as critical subject beyond all reason, much like how Adorno deems art a grotesque, inflated 'absolute commodity' with no use-value in place to stop it from expanding to whatever the market will bear.[28] Only an intractable emphasis on labour, its potentials, limits and contradictions, can check the infinite expansion of the 'automatic subject'[29] of capitalist value in art as elsewhere. Such acts of emancipatory, feminist deflation occur

26 Ray Brassier, 'Foreword', in Mattin, *Social Dissonance*, Falmouth: Urbanomic, 2021, xv.

27 Helmut Draxler and Fraser's project *Services* (1994–7) could likewise be noted as an approach to a worker's inquiry without a workplace, albeit with a passion for the institution von Osten and her cohort could never muster.

28 Theodor W. Adorno, *Aesthetic Theory*, translated by Robert Hullot-Kentor, London: Continuum, 2007, 28.

29 Karl Marx, *Capital: A Critique of Political Economy, Volume I*, translated by Ben Fowkes, London: Penguin, 1992, 256.

repeatedly in the von Osten archive, and they provide a basis for thinking critique in a quite different sense to the one with which we have become familiar, as the self-reflexive and ultimately self-affirming property of the art institution, its spontaneous discourse of accountability.

3.

Infrastructure, Interrupted

The institution should not be safe as long as we are not safe.
Decolonize This Place

Over the last few years, while thinking about how theories of social reproduction can link the work of second-wave feminist artists to others from that period who may not have identified as such, I started to develop some still rather unsystematic thoughts on what I have been calling 'reproductive realism'. With this category, I try to think about contemporary art practices that are market-affirmative (sometimes market-reflexive, but not always) yet call upon the legacies of Marxist feminism, autonomist Marxism, queer and trans theory and politics to propose a theory of the subject and the collective as always already 'subsumed', that is, incorporated or co-opted into a flat horizontal plane (perhaps modelled on social media networks) of something called the production or the capture of value. It is a market realism with the vocabulary of social reproduction feminism, but one that really does understand reproduction, practically, as the reproduction of what is, and with only a representational (at times, purely academic or discursive) relation to alterity or negativity towards the status quo. What interests me about this approach is the performative gesture towards the futility of critique and the importance of reproduction (of life, of sociality, of queer kinship), with the former presented as abstract and destructive, and the second as a politics of survival truly adequate to the current moment of all-pervasive capitalist crisis, whether understood as a crisis of social reproduction, or a crisis of valorisation. While many examples could be brought to bear here – my own thinking along these lines began with my initially collaborative relation to a scene of queer and feminist post-internet art exhibition and discourse whose main protagonists went in a direction of non-ironic mimicry of art market functionality, under the auspices that critique was for the privileged – there is a cultural logic that is quite pervasive, one that splits the social field into two: those without privilege whose eyes are fixed only on the immediate, and the privileged who can afford to dream.

We see the relevant attitude encapsulated in this quote from a film review of the US film *The Florida Project*, which depicts the life of a six-year-old girl and her single mother in a budget motel near Disney World, Florida: 'Though Moonee and her friends do express slivers of their hopes and dreams, they keep their eyes down toward the grass, whereas children from wealthier backgrounds may look to the sky.'[1] The implication seems to be that the excluded can do all the working, but the rich are doing all the dreaming, and our everyday nightmares are their dreams, and that's just how it is. Though perhaps not intentional, there is a striking note of class contempt in such formulations, a total dismissal of any agency other than the reproductive in the notion that a radical reckoning with the way things are means making the best of them and no more.

So how does this relate to infrastructural critique, or to the drift from institution to infrastructure outlined in the last chapter? A thought very commonly articulated within the framework of 'reproductive realism' *qua* artistic anti-politics is that

1 Kaila Philo, 'Paradise Lost', *New Inquiry*, 16 January 2018, thenewinquiry.com.

all money is dirty, that complicity is unavoidable, and that, consequently, we should appropriate as much of it as possible, from whomever we can. When understood like this, the phrase argues in favour of an institutional status quo. Rather than a demoralisation (or rather, demystification) of material relations, which it plainly also is, it underwrites an attitude of complete licence. But while it is possible for the phrase to be received in just those terms, the epigraph from Decolonize This Place seems to advance a different perspective, suggesting that *vulnerability* is the connecting thread between communities and the art institution. Then the question becomes more strategic: the source of funds and the conditions of 'the public' itself are situated within a striated continuum of structural violence, over which no cloak of privacy can be draped. And this idea – that it's not the 'nature' of money that's relevant, but what it's used to do – can then be used to make some important distinctions: all money is dirty, but some of it is made from war crimes, or investing in funds that support ecologically genocidal industries, for instance. This is what *this* money was used to do, this is where it came from.

Here, a distinct aspect of infrastructural critique begins to come into view, as a way to connect an analysis of institutions, that is, organisations, to organising. The metaphorical 'dirt' attaching to money, like so many metaphors, doesn't say enough in the attempt to say it all. A recognition of the compromised character of the art institution may well represent an initial shredding of the modesty barrier between the money and the art, but determining how it matters and to whom is not a matter of principle – a moralistic exposure of a mismatch between the real and the ideal – but *a matter of struggle*, by artists and cultural workers, and also the 'non-cultural' workers deep inside any institution and the people organising on its outside as well. This means approaching the organisation, which means the art institution as well, from the viewpoint of the resources it contains and controls in an expanded sense, in contact and solidarity with other sites and movements. My interest is in developing a mode for critique that is not only dedicated to creating awareness of these (infrastructural) conditions of its own enunciation and the classed and racialised conditions of the critical encounter, especially in the institution of art, but a critique that makes cuts and lets in air, a critique that takes it upon itself to find or make the holes through which this infrastructure comes into view. And maybe these holes, whether incised by art or political organising, can be extended to enable a grasping and a torsion to be exercised on those conditions, tugging them into really completely different shapes if necessary, demolishing or abolishing them if not? All money enabling the art institution may be dirty, but what could we do with the money if it was really ours, with its power over us severely diminished? And the 'we' of 'ours' – who would draw this line around us, and how?

When the dumbwaiter breaks down

We have already briefly mentioned the conception of infrastructure as that which repeats – as a sunk cost, an operation by the past on the present, limiting the range of possible choices or outcomes and extending in linear fashion into the future. Here, critique enters through a temporal cut, which reorients or disfigures the smoothness of the line. Temporality and infrastructure, however, are entangled in ways that can be generalised beyond this particular scheme. Recalling the Kantian argument that space and time are the intuitions that make cognition in general possible, it seems that time could be defined both as an infrastructure and as something made of infrastructure.[2] But making our incision into the topic at this level of abstraction propels us almost immediately to a much more prosaic thesis, which brings the transcendental down to the empirical. The shift in scale, rather than kind, reminds us of another categorical pairing, the virtual and the actual, neither of which carries a lesser share of reality than the other.[3] The repetition is normalised into everyday routine, and, when it stops functioning, an aperture is cut into its artifice – through which history and power relations can be seen. Think of the global financial crisis; think of the water disasters in Flint or Detroit. The transcendental repetition is abstract (capitalism, class contempt, anti-Black racism) and the infrastructural repetition is found in the material conditions of possibility (captive regulations, lead pipes, privatised governance) that sustain social relations in a particular shape over time.

To say that infrastructure 'repeats' means that it works to enable a set of activities, and it works because the preconditions of its effectivity are neither visible nor relevant; these jut out when the infrastructure breaks down or if one element is isolated from the whole. The architecture theorist Reinhold Martin illuminatingly discusses infrastructure as a regime of intelligibility in terms that echo Michel Foucault's 'epistemes', but with a more concrete mediation of the social with the technological: 'The dumbwaiter, bound to slave labor, carries bottle after bottle up to Jefferson's dining room. Its systemic properties tend to become visible only when the repetitions cease. If the wine ceases to appear, at some level and only for an instant, the entire apparatus of slavery comes into view. When you turn on the faucet

2 See Immanuel Kant, *Critique of Pure Reason*, translated by Paul Guyer and Allen W. Wood, Cambridge: Cambridge University Press, Doctrine of Elements, Part 1, 167.

3 Gilles Deleuze, *Difference and Repetition*, 183ff.

and water does not flow, the entire water system leaps into the cognitive field.'[4]

Broken infrastructure is loquacious. 'Institutions of negation', a term that Suhail Malik uses to categorise labour organisations, art workers' coalitions and radical social movements, certainly need the affirmative moment that is infrastructure. And yet the reproductive aspect of infrastructure also has to retain an openness to the 'temporal cut' that undoes crystallisations and institutions in the attempt to realise the desires that were the initial impetus for their establishment.[5] Infrastructure might be that which repeats, but this repetition is not without difference: it can monotonously produce the same differences (such as infrastructures that reproduce social inequalities), but it can also be a means of ensuring the reproduction of a wholly different form of social life over time. Martin's example of the dumbwaiter illustrates the complexity of this situation, because the breakdown in the machinery reveals a system of slave labour that is also capable of bringing the apparatus to a halt on its own terms – a move that rules out the treatment of infrastructure and labour as though they were simply *categorically* distinct. But how to develop a vocabulary supple enough to think their interrelations, which is to say, to describe their entanglement both within art and transversally to it?

The challenge will here be taken up first in connection with some work by the artist Dora Budor, who frequently focuses on the architectural infrastructure of the exhibition space, and then with some recent labour struggles in the art field. I argue it is infrastructure's transversal character – between the material and

4 Isabelle Graw, Reinhold Martin and André Rottmann, 'Do Media Determine Our Situation? Reflections on the Transatlantic Reception of Friedrich Kittler', *Texte zur Kunst*, 98 (June 2015), 76.

5 Malik, 'Art's Exit from Contemporary Art'.

the possible, between machines and working drawings, between cognitive maps and the terrain they depict – that enables it to ask political questions that can no longer be replied to in the abstract, either with the false totalisation of exit or the demobilising complicity of what I call reproductive realism.

Fluids and negative spaces

We are accustomed to thinking of metamorphosis as an animating principle for art-making. Transformation of one form into another, division and multiplication of forms, and/or displacements around the invisible force field between an object and an art object are essentially how we understand art to function. It's a 'manifest image' – that is, both a point of departure and a misdirection. What we think before we've started thinking. The matter-form dialectic underpinning this framework would later turn into the form/content division, before even this heuristic became unbearably basic, in a time no one remembers any more. But I would suggest that this heavily caveated micro-history of form involves a mis- or non-recognition of another means, a path of errancy when it comes to form and its wavering possibilities. This could be called the metamorphosis of gaps. Gaps rather than voids, for instance, because a void already hypostatises its emptiness as completeness, whereas a gap subsists in relation. A void is thus always aspiring to the status of an object, whereas a gap is cut into time, or language. It's a spacing that telescopes in and out of an (infra)structure, and may give an impetus for connecting beyond it.

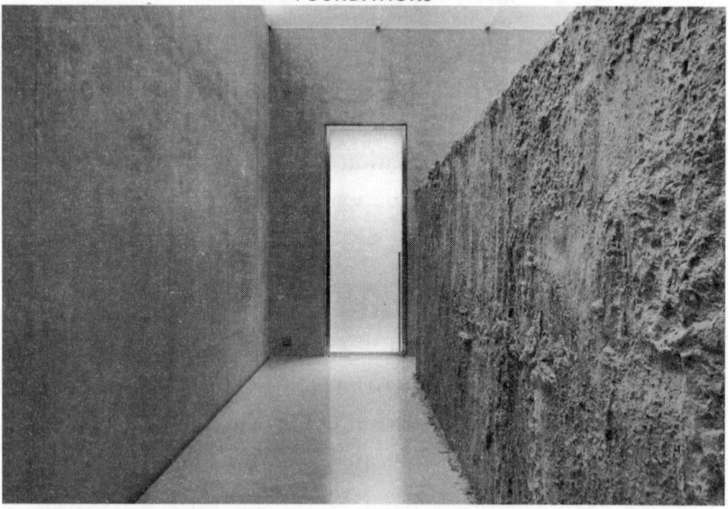

Dora Budor, *Kollektorgang (XV–XXIV)*, 2021. Installation view, Continent, first floor Kunsthaus Bregenz, 2022. Photo by Gina Folly. Courtesy of the artist © Dora Budor, Kunsthaus Bregenz

The artist and writer Dora Budor works to generate such a transformation of gaps and significant absences. We can think of the gap as the errancy of a system – the negativity at the core of its positive appearance or structural integrity in the world.[6] A few key models for this thinking of the gap here could be Achille Mbembe's concept of 'necropolitics'; Ursula K. Le Guin's tale of the tortured child in the basement that enables all civil society to flourish ('The Ones Who Walk Away from Omelas' [1973]); or Frank B. Wilderson III's analogue to this figure in political theory, the prison slave in a world predicated on anti-Blackness.[7] These

6 See Endnotes, 'Error', in *Bad Feelings*, London: Bookworks, 2016.

7 Achille Mbembe, *Necropolitics*, Durham: Duke University Press, 2019; Ursula K. Le Guin, 'The Ones Who Walk Away from Omelas', in *The Wind's Twelve Quarters*, New York: Harper & Row, 1975; Frank B. Wilderson III, 'The Prison Slave as Hegemony's (Silent) Scandal', *Social Justice*, 30, 2 (2003).

are all translations into the idiom of social death and biopolitical oppression of a certain familiar 'logic of the supplement' – the exception that sustains the rule but cannot be thought within the rule at the cost of the coherence of the rule and the world that it justifies.[8] The negativity of this supplement can be thought of as primarily terminal, as in the death or deprivation enabling any project of plenitude or development, or as speculative, as a space incubating possible forms in all their virtual actuality. It is the manner in which these gaps are produced, whether by cuts or other means, that allows us to think of them as constitutive, as models for thought or a speculative approach to infrastructures just as stolid – if not solid – as an excavation pit in which a building stands, of the kind we see presented in Budor's works *Kollektorgang (I–XIV)*, *Kollektorgang (XV–XXIV)* and *Kollektorgang (XXV–XXIX)*, a series of sculptures intended by the artist 'as both monuments and obstructions' (see photo above). These expose or invert the underground diaphragm walls of their exhibition space, originally intended to prevent the collapse of surrounding buildings as well as to form a collector duct for internal seepage. The fluids and negative spaces of the Kunsthaus Bregenz are thus coaxed out by the artist and take different solid forms, as if encouraging the building to heal by 'acting out' in a kind of object therapy. The building as a body, coughing up very indexical hairballs, could be one way of describing the casted ducts she has produced.

With Budor's *Love Streams* (2022) you get a kind of externalisation, as medications are crushed into material, a form of 'acting out' in a psychoanalytic sense, opposed to medicated passivity. A distant analogue here could be Karla Black's

8 Jacques Derrida, *Of Grammatology*, corrected ed., translated by Gayatri Chakravorty Spivak, Baltimore: Johns Hopkins University Press, 1997, 7.

blow-up application of makeup as pigment on surfaces and spaces, like Budor attracted by the capacity of unexpected substances to flesh out links between body, psyche and structure. Or, to bring the thought of externalisation to the *Kollektorgang* walls, it arranges for absences to perform differently, as well as change form. It is not just the evoked absence of the below-ground duct that is surfaced here, but also the paper-crete that clads these forms – shredded office paper that may or may not have had a secretive function but certainly signified something else and played a role that can never be reconstructed from the form it has taken in the weird branch of the 'circular economy' represented by contemporary art. This salience of the psycho-analytic, the shifting of back and front stages of performativity that extends it to a behavioural psychology of stuff and gaps, means that the corporeal and the political don't need to be parallel routes to pursue in detachment from one another, but only make sense in each other's folds. There's a clear indication that this kind of activation has ties to Budor's training in architecture and the interest in set design that accompanied her shift into film and theatre early on in her trajectory. If the significance of the gap is understood politically – that it has dimensions moving outwards from just what it can offer to a nimble artistic process – then its capacity to generate absences of different shapes (and bulks, and stances, and compositions, and odours) becomes a compelling project.

To take just one piece, such as the *Kollektorgang* walls, Budor locates different forms of absence, the different ways absence functions, and finds ways of materialising this absence. Some variation of casting can be involved (*Something to Remind Me*, 2020; 27 *Male Molds*, 2021), where a negative space generates a panoply of forms at a range of scales, contrasts and genres (from engagement ring to chain link to bicycle wheel, from metal mould to side table, from foundation pit to sculptural room divider). A 'non-identity' of the original space can also be flushed out to the surface in the transmutation between infrastructure and art, as a negative space doesn't just hold emptiness. A space can also be a sponge or 'collector duct' for water, keeping it from causing damage to the iconic Kunsthaus Bregenz building – a building whose mystique derives from its continuous fabric. Likewise, a building where light circulates through techniques other than windows is a building that it makes sense to animate with the sound of concealed vibrators emanating from discreet slits between wall and floor (*Termites*, 2022). The constructivist instinct between architecture and surrealism often also invokes recessive or decayed industrial forms. This is evident in a number of the works, cited previously, in the *Continent* exhibition in Bregenz, 021's *Autoreduction* exhibition at Progetto in Lecce, or the *Autophones* (2022) piece Budor contributed to the 59th Venice Biennale. For the latter, the gap in the piece is, once again, an industrial artefact, this time an artefact key to Venice's military shipbuilding past – the air hammer, a tool whose name collides action and absence, disclosing the artist's craft-wise approach to metaphysics, as well as the erotic guile of her enclosures: here, again, the gap emits a sex-toy buzz. Nothing is simply a self-sufficient work or a needy prop; everything has a secret.

Biopolitics is a clear focus in Budor's discovery and activation of these gaps. The appearance of spaces and openings versus the need to present a solid, impermeable front is a recurrent theme in the analysis of the relation between gender normativity and political reaction. Klaus Theweleit's singular book *Male Fantasies* (1977–8) spelled out the thesis as he read the journals and propaganda of the pre–World War II German fascist militias, with their horror of fluids, filth and communist women, while, more recently, the poet and writer Danny Hayward revived this inquiry in his reflections on 'gaplessness' and the 'block' as the body-ideal of far-right affect: 'Fascists imagine themselves as blocks because the idea that their personalities might contain holes or gaps is unbearable to them. They need to be impenetrable, complete, positively constipated with their own heroism.'[9] Right-wing pathos trembles pleasurably at the thought of a solid body, a body that can never be disassembled and only ever gets bigger. The idea that the body may only change in the limited sense of infinite expansion of the same echoes pitifully in the economic rhetoric of one of the more recent glitching avatars to run the British state, with her anathemas on the 'lens of redistribution "over" growth'. It could also cast another light, you might say, on the right-wing agitation against 'critical' school curricula in the United States. A terror of gaps and spaces where difference or doubt might creep into the solid, normal block that every schoolchild would otherwise present. Opening up unsanitary gaps where new knowledge could get in. This paranoid intimation aligns with the notion of critique at issue in 'infrastructural critique' as the forcing of gaps or 'cuts' in the existent that might provide not just glimpses of but access to other possibilities. Whereas the organic whole is the pathos-structure of domination, the identity-thinking key to nationalisms and fundamentalisms of all kinds. And non-identity can only be evoked – never directly attained – through the critique of identities reproduced by the brute force of exchange, the transactions and extractions driving capitalist society.

In trying to build an infrastructural milieu for Budor's practices, I try to think of artists who poeticise or pattern voids into significant structure. Two figures shift into place like colour gels, highlighting and changing my impressions of Budor's recent

---

9 Klaus Theweleit, *Male Fantasies*, 2 vols, translated by Stephen Conway et al., Minneapolis: University of Minnesota Press, 1987–9; Danny Hayward, '"Language Is for Fucking Idiots": On Porpentine Charity Heartscape', in *Wound Building: Dispatches from the Latest Disasters in UK Poetry*, Goleta: Punctum Press, 2021, 176.

work. One is Méret Oppenheim's furry cup known as *Object* (*Le Déjeuner en fourrure*, 1936), with its antic luxuriousness of the void, both empty and upholstered – a pause in an animal. The other is Matthew Angelo Harrison, who fills voids in machine-printed resin with equally machine-printed traditional African sculpture, populating the original primitivist void of modernism with state-of-the-art industrial tech, cutting what he calls the two sides of modernism – 'semblance of purity' and 'instrument of oppression' – against one another as a single fused juxtaposition. This is likewise a playing of material and socio-historical voids off one another. At the limits of the artistic 'field', Budor's perforated surrealism also invokes other kinds of infrastructural critique – architectural, economic, linguistic, organisational. Her *Autoreduzione*, for example, conjures Italian social-reproduction struggles in Lecce, once dominated by a heavily feminised and militant tobacco workforce, now by an agritourism complex that includes enterprises such as boutique hotels and art spaces. The tabacchine of Lecce didn't just have the bosses to reckon with. The action taken by women workers, as the Italian autonomist feminists put it, was a 'struggle within the struggle' – which is, perhaps, itself one way of thinking infrastructural struggles in general.

Concrete universals

Adorno argued that art both reflects and rejects the forces of production of its era. If we find ourselves living in an era of economic stagnation, an era when the resurgence of violence and direct extraction are the engines of accumulation, how does this register in the ways in which artistic labour deploys its own practical exceptionality, as a form of social praxis? Perhaps the speculative force of labour politics in the field of art could help us to think this, rather than the transformation of artistic labour per se. Labour politics would here appear as non-art, as 'foreign matter', but by the same token as force of negation. A transversal current that links up with social movements not strictly in the field of art could be capable of pushing art further, both conceptually and politically. Such a push would rely on its powers of infrastructural critique, which is to say a critique that starts making other spaces and structures for practice even as it diagnoses the problems with existing ones.

The analysis of labour in art should be undertaken with a negative (critical) scope, rather than an affirmative one. This goes for labour politics in general, insofar as they represent one aspect of a revolutionary orientation towards the present – 'revolutionary' in the sense of taking up the perspective of the overcoming of this present. This is no doubt a both/and issue, since, as I argued before, organising around material conditions of injustice requires affirmative moments for anything like a counter-vision to the existing order to take root among large groups of people who are conditioned both professionally and socially to see themselves as individuals, in competition for scarce resources in a 'meritocratic' market. Labour in art thus instantiates a form of 'double consciousness': it affirms itself as an organising tactic in a field that denies it, but it also contests itself, as well as the field of art, as an aspect of its speculative force. Labour politics in art have to overcome both labour and art, which per Adorno is institutionalised as the anti-matter of labour.

One moment of artistic class struggle with an infrastructural dimension took place in 2018 at what was then my own workplace, in the blockade of the opening of the Goldsmiths Centre of Contemporary Art, as part of the Justice for Workers student and staff solidarity campaign for the struggle of cleaners to be 'in-housed' by the university (see photo on facing page). Here, the

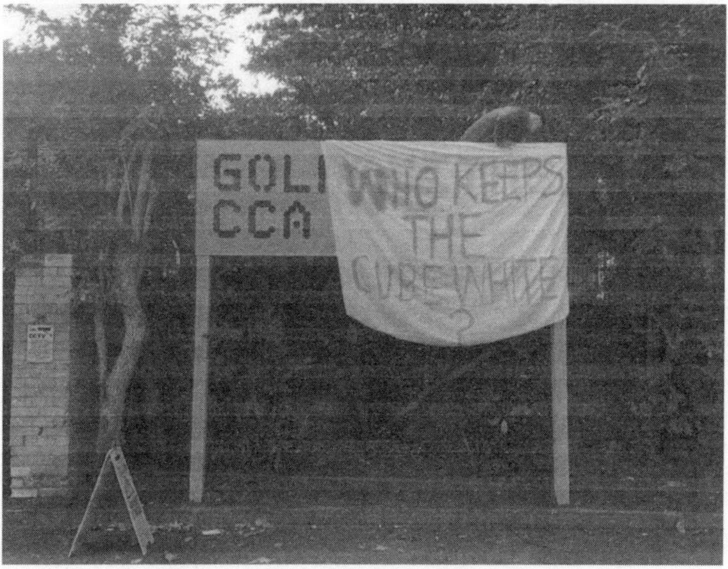

Justice for Cleaners, Who Keeps the Cube White Demonstration, 2018. Image © Goldsmiths Cleaners

precarious, racialised workforce whose labour was necessary for the reproduction of the institution linked up with artists and art students to reveal the dependency of Goldsmith's growth strategy – a new gallery space, featuring an opening exhibition 'about' the politics of work – on their own degraded working conditions. Another example can be found in the coordination between activist groups campaigning against current manifestations of the military-industrial complex that supports art institutions, exhibiting artists and the workers in art institutions. An instance of this is the significant case of Warren Kanders and the Whitney Biennial in New York, which is different again from the somewhat similarly motivated Sydney Biennale boycott of 2014, called by the exhibiting artists and not initially by a coalition.

In all these campaigns, the need for a coalition seems pretty basic. However, it's not always clear from a lot of the activism in and around art institutions in recent years, including eco-activism, that the coordination of different groups is necessarily sought or even desired. Perhaps workers are tacitly willing to stand aside and let protests take place, as in the action of the protest group BP or Not BP? at the British Museum, and perhaps there are concerns about exposing workers to managerial retribution with too-visible forms of coordination on the part of activist groups. But, most of the time, the conditions and demands of institutional employees, who are frequently super-precarious or indirectly employed, are not part of the campaigns targeting the atrocious investments and alliances that characterise powerful cultural institutions.

This raises a problem that has been central to a great deal of my previous work. If there is anything systematic about my thinking, it is the project of developing a non-functionalist, non-ontological and dialectical understanding of the constitutive status of the exception to the operation of the rule in the capitalist totality (the *concrete* universal of what is a structurally or tendentially totalising and never complete totality). Art is one of the most obvious of these constitutive exceptions, and a lot of the ambiguity regarding the labour of the artist has to do with the structure and organisation of this labour, with how it is deemed to be so different from other kinds of labour that it cannot be regulated or provide a ground for organising in anything like the same way that other kinds of labour do. This stems from the assumption that non-artistic labour is 'homogeneous', as opposed to the incalculable particularity of artistic labour. Yet this is hardly the case when the dominant trends of hyper-fragmentation and the precarity of contracts and conditions are taken into account, from the gig economy of food delivery to the gig economy of academia. These differences are also at the root of the disavowal of labour in art – hence the super-exploitation of this labour, as in any other field where collective or structural conditions are mystified or hidden. The basis of this mystification is the resistance to recognising the artist as a subject of labour or to including the artist among other cultural workers whose labour is often waged, albeit lightly regulated. Both of these exclusions are premised on the wilful refusal to separate artistic work from artistic labour – that is, to separate art as an activity from the working conditions in the field – and thus, ultimately, the refusal to see one's work and one's activity as imbricated in power relations along an axis of responsibility and negation, or in other words, in shared conditions that can serve as a basis for political organisation.

Common approaches to art and labour protect the threatened status of 'autonomous' artistic subjectivity, which many in the field have been educated and socialised to believe is exceptional and an escape route from meaningless forms of employment. This may be the reason why, when artists find themselves in labour situations with the humdrum characteristics of service, standardisation and exploitation that they had sought to escape by going into the arts, they often don't identify with these situations enough to do anything about them. This is increasingly true for non-artists as well, and is a mindset very difficult to shed, regardless of the political contents of any artistic work that is being produced. Because the autonomy of art is a social institution with material effects, it is not a personal belief or sectoral ideology that individuals may or may not choose to adopt – it is an infrastructural condition. Autonomy is the feedstock of precarity.

And this is why the contested autonomy of art is structurally similar to the realised autonomy of financialised capital.[10] We need to distinguish between the labour of the artist as author and all the other kinds of labour included in the social materiality of art, as well as in the technical or institutional conditions for the circulation of art, from fabrication to exhibition to pedagogy. But then the question of the technical and political composition of art also

10 Vishmidt, *Speculation as a Mode of Production*, ix ff.

emerges, as in the class-composition analysis developed by autonomist Marxism. Briefly, the technical composition of a field refers to how the field is organised institutionally and economically, whereas its political composition represents the potential to reorder or refuse those conditions.[11] Because there are many ways to articulate the politics of artistic labour, the act of 'calling out' the invisibility of labour in the field of art, as with any other injustice or element of structural – and structuring – violence, is not useful if this is the extent of the intervention, hoping only to regulate an intolerable situation. If that approach is limited by its gesturality, however, the politics of artistic labour do not need to be thus limited when strategies of transversality can be developed and deepened with other workers (horizontally) and with the dominant conditions of accumulation and value in the field (vertically). Both these directions describe class struggle in the field of art.

This brief summary of the role of labour in art raises another, related question: how does the labour of cultural workers reproduce both the physical and the 'social and moral element' of art institutions? As was the case at Goldsmiths, this problem could provide a basis for cultural workers to coordinate their efforts with those of socially reproductive workers operating in wholly different coordinates of race, class and social status – namely, service workers whose reproductive labour is not even mystified, just constantly degraded. Certainly, a discussion cannot be had in a space characterised by its attention to the ethical, as the artworld purports to be, about what prospects a more material politics have 'in wider society', if these politics do not address related injustices closer to home. The conditions of this wider society are, of course, reflected in the working conditions and

11 For an overview of this tendency in Marxism, see Steve Wright, *Storming Heaven: Class Composition and Struggle in Italian Autonomist Marxism*, 2nd ed., London: Pluto, 2017.

representational moves of the art world, as has been abundantly evidenced by unionising campaigns in Western art institutions in recent years, as well as by these institutions' paper-thin commitments to racial justice, further exposed by the performative gestures following the George Floyd rebellion. In the liberal infrastructure of political thinking, or feeling, perhaps, in the institution of art, labour struggles are considered to be narrow and particular rather than to be instances of a concrete universal.[12] I argue that the generalisation of precarity can make these kinds of coordination both more politically obvious and more materially difficult to realise.

What do these tendencies represent and what can they tell us about the prospects for cultural worker organising as an element of infrastructural critique? The first lesson seems to be an admission: that serious labour organising within capitalist relations of production and power cannot start from the anomaly, but only from commonality. More precisely, a focus on the anomaly *qua* anomaly leads to a reformist trajectory, which is to say, petitioning to be included in the supposedly normal conditions of exploitation represented by a contract as a goal, rather than as a baseline. And the politics associated with that trajectory will have to be representational, since they will be driven by an advisory body and empowered individuals, rather than a transversally coordinated group of people organising around their shared material interests. The shift from the idea of organising as artists to organising as arts workers in relation to an employer seems to be propelled by the inefficacy of anomaly-based reformism, leading workers to turn towards unionisation as the 'baseline' for more radical reforms – a more traditional opening to radical horizons through reformist means. But it's a turn that is likely

12 On 'concrete universals', see 'Dialectics and anti-Dialectics', in *Marina's Cues*, edited by Kerstin Stakemeier, forthcoming 2027.

also prompted by a worsening political and economic climate of austerity, exacerbated by pandemic and war, as well as increasingly unchecked violent and racialised exploitation, undertaken in the name of 'reproductive realism' by the same arts institutions that engage in ameliorative gestural politics around representation and inclusion, as fashion dictates. The second lesson to be learned is, perhaps, that the infrastructure of exploitation that necessitates organising as workers cannot be fully engaged or dismantled without confronting the structural violence that the infrastructure both unleashes and cloaks – which is the racialised, gendered and abled forms in which class is lived, thus thoroughly shaping the labour relation. Hence, art institutions become a hyper-visible target, but also a resource for the convocation of various movements approaching the leviathan from different related and implicated directions – which could imply Budor's elliptical but forceful surrealism just as easily as the kinds of practical interruption of the arts infrastructure just described.

And, with this, we return to the question of gaps – between the formal and the practical, between different classes of workers, between the 'mission' of the institution and its everyday reality – as places where an infrastructural critique can intervene. In Part 2 of this book we propose ways of thinking these different movements *in relation*, orienting ourselves towards a 'negative totality' that would situate the logics of gender, race and normativity within the form of value.[13] The limits of what the institution is

13 On 'negative totality', see Zoe Sutherland and Marina Vishmidt, '(Un)making Value: Reading Social Reproduction Through the Question of Value', in *Totality Inside Out: Rethinking Crisis and Conflict Under Capital*, edited by Kevin Floyd, New York: Fordham University Press, 2022; and, among his various writings on this subject, Chris O'Kane, 'The Path of Negative Totality: From the Critique of Political Economy to a New Reading of the Critical Theory of The Negative Totality of Capitalist Society', jjay.cuny.edu.

able to incorporate or include are also the points at which institutional critique passes into the key of abolition, disclosing the infrastructural neutrality of the great majority of critical artistic practices as always and only a weapon of the propertied, and arts institutions as just another site of accumulation whose ideological and actual capital has to be dismantled and redistributed as part of a process of generalised, as well as specific, social antagonism. 'It should not be safe as long as we are not safe.'

Part II.

Crystal Drills

4.
Reproduction

In the general project of infrastructural critique, much of the work I have been doing over the years has been related to displacing the boundaries between production and its conditions. The attempt to shift the standpoint from institutions to infrastructure stemmed from a concern that institutional critique was too invested in preserving the frame as a condition of its legitimacy. Citing Olga Goriunova, we could say that the foregrounding of 'organisational mediations' as the content of the artwork echoes the question of construction in Adorno's aesthetics – what he called 'the plenipotentiary of logic and causality transferred to the artwork from the domain of objective knowledge' – while pushing the material, and materialist, envelope of how such construction is to be defined.[1] By being shifted into an infrastructural register, the conservative implications of an epistemology-heavy institutional critique (again, the Kantian question *what can I know*, given the conditions of the field and myself as an agent within it? How is this knowledge legitimated?), along with the ethical arguments that so often accompany it, are annulled, in favour of an inquiry that is at once more empirical and more practical. More empirical, because the question is oriented towards material 'affordances' – what materials constitute the artwork's conditions of possibility? What is it and where is it? – and more grounded,

1 Olga Guriunova, 'Participatory Platforms and the Emergence of Art', in *A Companion to Digital Art*, edited by Christiane Paul, London: Blackwell, 2016; Adorno, *Aesthetic Theory*, 57.

because the inquiry takes the standpoint of praxis – what organisational and economic conditions need to be in place for this to acquire the status of an artwork? What can be done to repurpose these conditions, or this status?

By thinking the frame as a location in a contested social field, along with the resources this makes available, the frame can be demystified, not just ideologically but materially. This has been an undertaking that has long proved central to feminist organising and theory, in whose Marxist variants the question of 'conditions' was always connected to the conditions *of reproduction*, that is to say, the work that is involved (gendered, unwaged, 'abject' or devalued) in creating the conditions in which other work (waged work, artwork) can appear and acquire value. In this chapter, I want to delve more deeply into this connection, and into the role of 'conditions' in infrastructural critique more broadly, by thinking about how the problems of reproductive labour are addressed in one strand of feminist art running from the 1960s into the present.

The two reproductions

In the midst of the current resurgence both in radical queer and trans feminism and other discourses and liberation movements that tactically affirm identity against its violent identifications by the state, such as Black Lives Matter, 'social reproduction' has gained traction as a key category beyond the field of Marxist feminism. This is largely because social reproduction appears to offer a certain flexibility in accommodating long-standing critiques of white middle-class hegemony in feminism, while returning to a more totalising framing than that afforded by the academically established discourses of intersectionality. Indeed, it is specifically within this expanded approach that a more global picture of diverse concrete positions of a population increasingly surplus to capital's valorisation requirements can be developed. Such a population, made surplus to as well as targeted by the necropolitical violence of today's accumulation imperatives, faces a real existential crisis in its ability to reproduce itself across its differentiated components. Here, social reproduction analysis approaches these positions in a specific way, treating them as devalued forms of labour in the current phase of capitalist accumulation. To this extent, it aligns with the approach to 'conditions' in infrastructural critique: it brings the conditions for capitalist reproduction into the frame.

A difficulty arises, however, when we ask what it is that is being reproduced. During the 1970s and early 1980s, Marxist feminists often emphasised the centrality of reproduction, arguing either that reproduction was value-producing in Marxist terms and/or that it constituted the conditions of possibility of the production of value. But the concept of social reproduction can often be stretched, designating not just the reproduction of a specific historical mode of production, but the reproduction of life per se, through which the capital relation is reproduced *as though contingently*. As such, it becomes difficult to explain what distinguishes the reproduction of the capital relation in any determinate sense. The Marxist-feminist concept of social reproduction can also mean something quite specific: the production and reproduction of the special commodity of labour-power ('special' because it adds more value in the production process than it costs).[2] Yet what falls within the remit of the reproduction of labour-power is itself still open to specification, given social, historical and geospatial difference. This is what makes it difficult conceptually to distinguish the reproduction of labour-power from the reproduction of life as such, particularly when what Michael Denning calls

2 Marx, *Capital, Volume I*, Chapter 6.

'wageless life' or other writers have called 'surplus population' – meaning surplus to capital's valorisation needs, becoming the redundant, the precarious, the expelled – becomes an experience more and more central to the configuration of global societies in an era of ongoing crisis.[3] Thus, social reproduction names 'a continuously changing [process] which expands and contracts both in response to its own internal dynamics, and under the pressure of the continuous attempts at enclosing it on the part of the capitalist machine'.[4]

Within the artworld, we see a reflection of some of these debates in discussions around the concept of 'care', which is sometimes invoked as if there were just one such thing and that the invocation of the word was enough to signal its nature. What we often see in this kind of thinking is a desire to separate reproductive labour from its position in the reproduction of capital – a common *telos* of the feminist politics of social reproduction, and one that can generate unwelcome effects, such as the moralising affirmation of care work, the self-evident necessity of crisis management and the undergirding of gender roles, none of which diverge in any radical way from capitalism's perennial strategies for extracting profit from those least able to sustain it. For me, developing the notion of 'speculation' over the past decade was in part an attempt to avoid this kind of moralisation, which ends up affirming the normativity of use value and labour in general, as ways of organising society and a position from which to critique it. Art is a speculative practice that is capable of ontologically,

3 Michael Denning, 'Wageless Life', *New Left Review*, 66, November/December (2010), newleftreview.org; Bue Rübner Hansen, 'Surplus Population, Social Reproduction and the Problem of Class Formation', *Viewpoint Magazine*, 31 October 2015, viewpointmag.com.

4 Fulvia Serra, 'Reproducing the Struggle: A New Feminist Perspective on the Concept of Social Reproduction', *Viewpoint Magazine*, 31 October 2015, viewpoint.com.

epistemologically and hopefully sometimes politically undermining the reproductive positivity of labour, helping to realise its negativity through another set of mechanisms.

The key question for infrastructural critique is, then, how to approach the conditions of reproduction in their gendered, racialised and colonial specificity without drawing from them an affirmative politics that valorises the 'subject of reproduction' and her activities.[5] This would entail neglecting the dialectic between the reproduction of life and the reproduction of capital in favour of a benign, 'autonomising' vision, as if life and capital can go their separate ways, each engaged in a dynamic of self-valorisation, unmediated by the state and its mechanisms of coercion and consensus. In seeking to preserve this dialectic, I have tried to distinguish consistently between two *forms* of reproduction, namely (1) the social reproduction that has visibly risen to the top of the agenda of materialist feminisms from Marxist to intersectional perspectives, that is, as a *specific* modality of gendered, racialised and often unwaged labour; and (2) social reproduction as the 'reproduction of the conditions of production' as discussed by Louis Althusser, which includes institutions of the state and civil society, such as schools, the church and art galleries.[6] This latter sense refers to the continuum between the reproduction of 'life' (the maintenance of individuals) and what is more generally categorised as 'the economic' (social production). What is at stake is an analytic distinction

5 See Marina Vishmidt, 'Known Nowheres: Some Short Thoughts on Going Beyond', in *Utopian Pulse: Flares in the Darkroom*, edited by Ines Doujak and Oliver Ressler, London: Pluto, 2015.

6 Louis Althusser, *On the Reproduction of Capitalism: Ideology and Ideological State Apparatuses*, translated by G. M. Goshgarian, Verso: London, 2014; see also 'Ideology and Ideological State Apparatuses', in *Lenin and Philosophy and other Essays*, translated by Ben Brewster, New York: Monthly Review Press, 2001 [1971].

between two forms that are both historically specific even as they often blur into one another or overlap. On the one hand, we have a historical analysis of the reproduction of labour that is assigned to different categories of people; on the other hand are the broad, 'biopolitical' requirements for the reproduction of life, including the institutions of art.

What do we avoid by means of this distinction? Mainly a perspective in which the reproduction of the population of workers blurs into the reproduction of the species per se, and the problem of reproductive tasks becomes entwined not only with the reproduction of the capitalist mode of production but also with humanity as such. What we *gain* is a method of approach that allows us to think reproduction in a more differentiated way. Among other things, it allows us to ask of historical and contemporary art practices whether they are readable in terms of a feminist optic of reproduction as a spectrum of gendered tasks, or rather perform the impasses of a kind of social 'non-reproduction' that belongs to the second type, with the social reproduction perspective acting as a type of institutional or, rather, infrastructural critique – bringing conditions into the frame. Reproduction, I will argue with reference to these practices, does not have to become ontologised or naturalised to be a generative source of artistic or political activity. If reproductive labour under capitalist conditions is a 'fate worse than death', because it reinforces the brutalities and instrumentalities of gender, race and accumulation in simply keeping things going and people alive, it can also be the logic of resistance on the way to a non-capitalist form of social organisation, in which maintenance and creativity, reproduction and production, can and should no longer be distinct.[7]

---

7 Endnotes, 'The Logic of Gender: On the Separation of Spheres and the Process of Abjection', *Endnotes*, 3 (2013), endnotes.org.uk.

In particular, it is to the negativity, waste and uselessness of reproductive labour we must turn in order to see the vulnerability at the level of the social whole in relation to which this work is both abjected and moralised, in the usual 'dialectic' of gender and racial hierarchy in class societies. Through this way of looking at 'reproduction' in art, I'd like to trace a politics of subjectivity that reflects both the strategic affirmations and the refusals of identity endemic to all movements of the oppressed, in which art in particular behaves as not simply a mediating institution but an *iterative* one, a reproductive institution in its own right: on the one hand, a site of inventive and self-determined forms of work, on the other, an institution traversed by struggles and exclusions and dependencies.

A reproductive allegory with seemingly depthless levels

This sets the scene for a discussion of art in which *conditions* are what is at stake. Since at least the 1970s, the denaturalisation of reproduction has been pursued by a number of art practices whose take on the 'conditions of reproduction' indexes a shift in the focus of systemic feminist critique, from the labour of the housewife in the 1970s to the dispersal of this focus among the 'infrastructures' that today determine the collective life chances of entire populations.

Why would we be interested in art here? The answers to that question come from a number of places. The relationship between production and reproduction has been a core issue for feminist art in recent decades and in the present – though one not consistently attended to by feminist art history. The depiction of working women or women's labour, in and out of the market, constitutes a strong strand in the image politics of feminist art and film, but there is another, perhaps more oblique strand. Here, the artist identifies with being a worker, but it is not clear whether their labour is productive, reproductive or totally *un*productive. Art like this raises a more specific question, about how to allegorise the entropic qualities of reproductive labour, denaturalising it by making it look foolish, futile or indeed grandly absurd.

The various denaturalisations of reproductive labour cut away its social embeddedness, showing it as an activity that can be de- and re-contextualised, while they highlight the social relationship within which this activity can either acquire or lose an aura of inevitability and necessity. Entropy seems like the main modality through which we experience alienation from the manifest or unarguable 'usefulness' of reproductive labour – 'a woman's work is never done' and so on. Nonetheless, we can start off here by regarding practices that take an infrastructural approach to the field of art to stake out an embodied, affective and formal critique of (non-)reproductive institutions, such as the carceral complex, racialised urban decline and the violence of physical and mental normativity. In these respects, the practices of Cameron Rowland, but also Park McArthur, LaToya Ruby Frazer and Eva Koťátková, reward close attention. In McArthur and Rowland's work especially, there is a co-extensive dimension of immanent critique of the art institution, yet one that both absorbs and inverts the laminated lessons of that approach. It is the contingency and the overdetermination of the art institution and not its omnipotence that we are shown when wheelchair access ramps are harvested from nearby facilities and reappear as works in McArthur's exhibition, or when rented prisoner-made desks are put up for rent rather than for sale – evoking the system of convict-leasing – in Rowland's shows. Stigmatised identity is articulated as a formal principle. Here, a reproductive focus implicates the art institution as a paradoxical 'state apparatus' that both normalises *and* defunctionalises, in Claire Fontaine's terms, allowing other potentials to emerge as material hypothesis.[8] However, like all institutions whose economic significance is displaced or relatively indirect, art can also act to legitimise existing social arrangements by providing a space of indeterminacy and experimentation.[9] Here, the question of what traction the defunctionalisation of subjectivities and objectivities can have, just like who does the work, cannot be deflected for long, which brings in the whole problematic legacy of institutional critique.

Going back in time and shifting category, the form of 'reproduction' that connotes 'reproductive labour' presents a more clear-cut strand in feminist art histories. The 1970s saw a number of feminist art strategies that operated to denaturalise both art and work from the standpoint of gender politics – emptying feminised domestic tasks of natural content to fill them with social content, in a way that also interrogated the normative aesthetic and institutional claims of art. Mierle Laderman Ukeles's 'Maintenance Art' dragged housework into the field of art, a canonical feminist gesture of naming 'life' as work that upended the sovereign unconditionedness of the artistic 'work' while exposing the gendered (and colonial) content of the principle of 'separate spheres' – of the public and the private, the economic and the domestic. Thus, like the 1970s political demand for Wages for Housework, Ukeles sought to valorise the excluded, here the excluded of the institution of art in its broadest sense, there of wage labour and the labour movement.

Here, the double movement of the artistic gesture, 'centring' reproductive labour while emptying it of content, mirrors the double movement of Wages for Housework itself, which, as was pointed out by its campaigners, was always simultaneously Wages

8 Claire Fontaine, *Human Strike Has Already Begun and Other Writings*, London: Mute, 2013, 8.

9 Vishmidt, *Speculation as a Mode of Production*, 9–10.

Against Housework.[10] In other words, it was always a 'transitional demand', a way to organise the movement and achieve the level of mobilisation at which the profound structural challenge posed by the demand to the wage relation – to capital as such – would become clear in practice. Like the basic income demand of today, the potentially revolutionary undertone of Wages for Housework is that it aimed to exceed the state's capacity to accommodate it. In both Ukeles's work and the political movement, we thus see that the valorisation is also a *de*valuing, that is, a strategy that also challenges the institution that orders visibility and invisibility, inclusion and exclusion, as well as the larger system it represents. This is the dynamic of affirmation and negation inseparable from all social movements as well as from the kind of politicised social practice for which Ukeles's work is often seen as the imprimatur.

We can also see that Ukeles introduced housework (or paid cleaning labour outside the home, as she does in other projects such as *Touch Sanitation* (1977–80) and *I Make Maintenance Art One Hour Every Day* (1976)) to the repertoire of feminist art as a comic medium; while, in terms of the 'reproduction of the relations of production', art's reproductive role in society is also highlighted thereby, and its sovereignty exposed to its own abjection, by associating it with these activities. Also from this era, though in a different register, we can mention the short performance films of Brazilian artist Leticia Parente, such as *In* (1975) and *Task I* (1982), which dwell on the fungibility between the gendered body and housework, between subject and object. Parente hangs herself up in wardrobes, lays herself on an ironing board to be ironed by her maid. Significantly, her location in the Brazilian post-colonial context meant that any dramatisation of gendered labour could

10 As the title of Silvia Federici's pamphlet originally had it. Silvia Federici, *Wages Against Housework*, Bristol: Falling Walls Network, 1975.

not help but disclose the racialised and classed 'Others' in the home, where much North American and Western European feminist art privileged the isolated 'housewife'.

Across these practices of staging, inversion and displacement, we also track gestures of negation. We see waste as creative force, as a medium that propagates the destruction of representation. Older references here could be Marcel Duchamp's 'dust breeding', the social reproduction of dust on his *The Bride Stripped Bare by Her Bachelors, Even (The Large Glass)* (1915–23) as itself a reproductive allegory with seemingly depthless levels. Ukeles's 'dust paintings' then consolidate this entropic tendency, even as the re-presentation of housework as art also points to an entropic loss at the level of art's 'heroic' signifying power – an ideology that persists undimmed where asseverations of uselessness and unproductivity are associated with gendered conventions of bohemian outsiderdom or solitary rebellion.

Dependencies

Yet the loss of this signifying power represents the point at which uselessness as bohemian self-assertion – a tendency still in evidence in some of the work from the 1990s discussed in Chapter 2 – is taken up and transformed into a more thoroughgoing investigation of thematics of insufficiency, need and dependency. At the same time, it represents the moment when reproduction sheds its moral self-evidence, allowing (infrastructural) dependencies to be approached beyond the limits of a perspective that in seeking to make 'reproduction' visible has sometimes emptied it of its historical and social content, naturalising it or equating it with life itself.[11]

11 For more extensive discussion of these topics, see Zoe Sutherland and Marina Vishmidt, 'Social Reproduction: New Questions for the

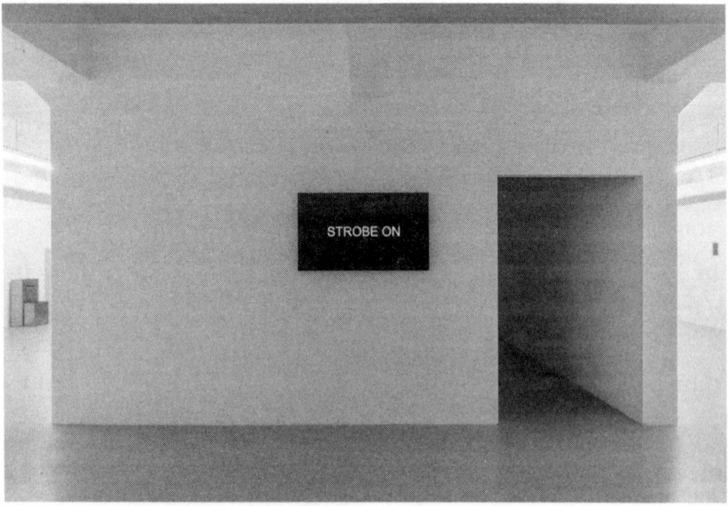

Carolyn Lazard, *Red*, 2021, Video installation, Kunstverein Braunschweig. Photo Stefan Stark.

In approaching the work of Ghislaine Leung and Carolyn Lazard in their respective contributions to *on affairs*, a group show at the Halle für Kunst Steiermark in 2022, we see some of the ways in which these tendencies play out in the present. Initially, the works appear to ask questions in an art historical register. Two historical truisms appear, asking to be dissolved. The first is the opposition between colour and line: *Browns* (2021) and *Red* (2021, see above) both generate a space, delineate it, through the deliberation of colour. The other is that conceptual art is opposed to relational art, because it is self-contained and tautological:

Gender, Affect and Substance of Value', *The New Feminist Literary Studies*, edited by Jennifer Cooke, Cambridge: Cambridge University Press, 2020. Also our 'Difference and the Universal in Legacies of Feminism', 2nd International Marxist Feminist Conference, Academy of the Fine Arts Vienna, 7–9 October 2016, youtube.com.

Leung and Lazard infuse the vocabulary of conceptualism with the materialism of dependency. The sketching out of an atmosphere through the delegated installation of industrial or quotidian objects, as in Leung's noise-cancelling *Fountains* (2022), also involves the production of space, or rather, its conditions (see below) – a gesture resonating with Lazard's *A Conspiracy* (2017), an installation of twelve ceiling-mounted white noise generators often found in healthcare and hospitality settings. The indeterminate status of objects between conditions and décor is perhaps not so new as a post-conceptual gesture, yet what these two practices, represented here by the first three works cited, accomplish, is a patterning of an exhibition space as a space of self-insufficiency.

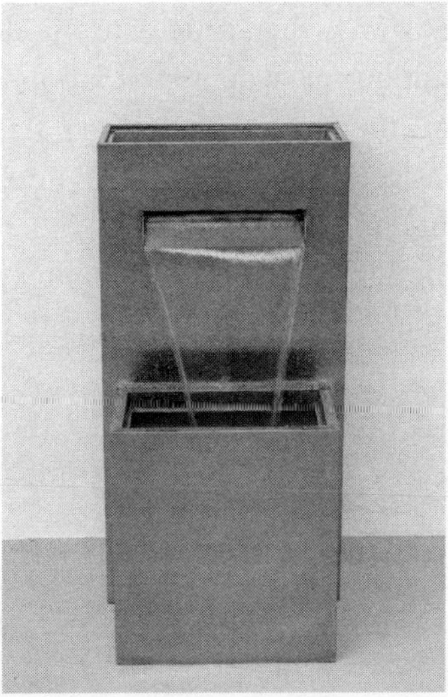

Ghislaine Leung, *Fountains*, 2022. A fountain installed in the exhibition space to cancel sound. Fountains, Halle für Kunst, Steiermark, Austria, 2023

For Lazard, this is a praxis that unfolds through questions around access in the exhibition space, here evoked by a switch from a potentially seizure-inducing flicker between black and white to red light, which pulsates more gently. Before even this can have its effects, however, a text in an anteroom of the exhibition space describes the potential experience for the viewer. The reference, Tony Conrad's *The Flicker* (1965), as well as Paul Sharits's films, is sublated from shock into an empathic gesture, minimalism no longer theatrical, as Michael Fried fretted in the 1960s, but perhaps a braver, if still equivocal phase-shift: minimalism as therapy. The way structural film literalises the conditions of the viewing experience is by bracketing everything that falls outside the phenomenological grain of the encounter between eye and moving image. Half a century later, Lazard unravels this by bringing the conditions for this bracketing into the picture. More than this, however, they articulate the dependency of the formal on its conditions as a matter of labour: the commingled labour of the artist, the curator, the gallery staff and the visitor. The labour is translated into access here, into information and adjustment, which combine to create an 'independent' artwork, modulating the time and space of the encounter in a different way, with its polemics (dependency) and autonomy (coherent gesture) tightly imbricated.

Lazard's work is often characterised by the proposition that the concept of 'access' can be used to formalise artistic labour itself, meaning that the conditions of access are enacted *within* artistic labour, rather than being dealt with as a mere afterthought. Their engagement with disability politics is what allows them such a specific vantage on the problem of labour conditions for not just the artist but the situation of art as such. Lazard's writings, work and advocacy over the past decade give us an insight not only into the daily impact of disability on a person with an art practice, but how chronic illness starts to undermine the very parameters of time and achievement imposed on young artists. Furthermore, it provides a view onto questions of access and accessibility that can be generalised to all kinds of conditions of limitation, such that they potentially constitute an ethics and a politics in themselves. Lazard is very clear that disability is a social condition, and one that, insofar as it deviates from capitalist understandings of health, individuality and productivity, can also serve as a ground to critique those understandings and to organise differently. An example of this is *Accessibility in the Arts: A Promise and a Practice*, which adopts the perspective that inclusion is not a special adaptation to some people who are less able to navigate conventional architectures and choreographies in art spaces, but a shift in how the audience–institution relationship is imagined, so that inclusion is inclusion for all – especially with disability as an eventual horizon for all.[12] This is a standpoint that has, in many cases, been integrated into policy, as is the case at my former workplace, Goldsmiths, where the standard assumption is that you work on making documents and lectures accessible for all, rather than adapting them to a minority who have specific 'needs'. This foregrounds the emergence of a consensus, to an extent, around the 'social model of disability', which recognises, as Lazard describes it, that, while impairment may be a physical or mental loss of function, disability is a relationship to the social and physical environment, which can be modified in such a way that it is easier for both disabled and non-disabled people to negotiate and confront the relegation of some bodies as not useful or appealing, needing to be excluded from public space as well as employment, education and other structures of survival in a capitalist economy.

The question of disability justice allows us to connect the ways in which labour appears and is practised in the field of contemporary art to issues around social reproduction in the broad sense

12 See Carolyn Lazard, *Accessibility in the Arts: A Promise and a Practice*, Philadelphia: Common Field, 2019, promiseandpractice.art.

that I have developed in this chapter. In particular, it helps us see how labour is gendered, racialised and naturalised until it is no longer visible as labour. At the same time, raising labour to visibility is not enough, if the working conditions are not seen to include both exploitation and oppression, which is to say that the conditions in which this labour is performed relies on its allocation to groups already deemed economically marginal and socially disposable. The social field is always already ethically striated. Raising the question from the standpoint of dis/ability and access means that injustice is located not simply in the fact that social reproduction becomes the responsibility of certain groups, but in the related and, at the same time, distinct reality of *what kind of society* and social relations are thereby being reproduced. Here, we come back to the trope of the two reproductions, as a way of thinking conditions in infrastructural critique.

In Lazard's earlier, more autobiographical text 'How to be a Person in the Age of Autoimmunity', they stake out their project of approaching disability – and the particular condition that they share with millions of other, predominantly feminised people, which is an autoimmune condition – through its implications for a broader analysis, one whose coordinates are socio-economic, political and affective.[13] Here, illness is seen as a biomedical and social condition at the same time, and one does not exclude the other. The biologically dysfunctional individual who just wants to get well and participate in society independently and the person produced as ill by a society because they fail to live up to its expectations are both actual and are dialectically entangled with one another. The situation is described by Lazard as a paradox, though it might also be thought of in the terms of Gregory Bateson as a 'double bind': that even as the ill

13 Carolyn Lazard, 'How to Be a Person in the Age of Autoimmunity' (January 2013), projectrowhouses.org.

person recognises that health and illness are social, not natural conditions, and that they can also serve to discipline the body in capitalist production (serving, in addition, as a vast source of profits within corporate healthcare systems), at the same time they want to be well.

An important part of Lazard's project is to see the body as an indicator or barometer of social ills, rather than a transparency to the soul, as they suggest with reference to a passage from Virginia Woolf. Even to have this conversation requires overcoming the shame and secrecy around being ill or disabled or differently abled in a society that values health, productivity and independence above all. It also means insisting on the relationality and contingency of the body against the self-defensive, military metaphors of everyday speech and medical science, as with the security metaphor of 'immunity' – but also of 'auto'.[14] They identify some of the ideological coordinates of this kind of metaphor by drawing an analogy between autoimmune disorder as the body attacking itself and capitalism as humans attacking their own conditions of survival, with the ecological consequences correlating with the enormous expansion over the last decades of autoimmune illnesses. They speak of this as the illness '[m]imicking, on a molecular level, the degrees of alienation and commodification that happen to the body on a social and economic level'. A recursive view, in other words. They also observe how people who otherwise identify as critical can mislay their scepticism when it comes to modern techno-medicine and show a marked lack of insight when it comes to disability.

'What happens when our bodies "revolt" and the factories stop functioning so smoothly? Perhaps they are trying to tell us

14 As an engagement with this history of autonomous aesthetics might suggest. See Kerstin Stakemeier and Marina Vishmidt, *Reproducing Autonomy: Work, Money, Crisis and Contemporary Art*, London: Mute, 2016.

something about their working conditions.'[15] Lazard revisits radical sickness politics as social movements, as with the 1970s German Socialist Patients Collective (SPK), with their critique of the 'medical-industrial complex' and demand for autonomy from the medical establishment. This should be understood in the sense of a historical left German extra-parliamentary politics – collective self-determination – rather than the insipid, formal autonomy of the liberal subject that may also be lurking within the 'auto' of autoimmunity. Here, the ideology is harder to dislodge than it normally is, since it has taken up residence in the double bind of health.

The accessibility guidelines Lazard develops in *Promise and Practice* elaborate the social model of disability in the pragmatic test case of cultural venues. The notes are titled 'a promise and a practice' to underline the prefigurative aspect of disability politics – that access is a horizon that needs to be worked towards and yet one that can already start to transform practices and relations in the present. This poses disability justice as a 'speculative practice' emerging out of real needs and conversations organised by the affected collectively through trial, error, offence and defence, rather than the imposition of government-drafted guidelines, for example, although the latter may also become the object of a demand. Lazard writes, 'Within this framework, disability is defined as an economic, cultural, and/or social exclusion based on a physical, psychological, sensory, or cognitive difference. Disability Justice movements understand disability to be unevenly distributed, primarily affecting Black and indigenous communities, queer and trans communities, and low-income communities. Disability is structurally reinforced by ableism, a system rooted in the supremacy of

15 Lazard, 'How to Be a Person in the Age of Autoimmunity'.

non-disabled people and the disenfranchisement of disabled people through the denial of access'.[16]

There is also an emphasis on the need for infrastructure – for the need to do infrastructure differently; that is, for infrastructural critique – that allows disabled artists and art workers, as well as audiences, to take part. Thus, arts institutions are not just spaces of representation but can actively support the lives and capacities of their participants: 'Supporting the cultural labour of disabled artists and thinkers must happen in tandem with infrastructural changes . . . There is often a striking discord between an institution's desire to represent marginalised communities and a total disinvestment from the actual survival of those communities. The ideal arts space is simple: it's one in which art and culture are not sequestered from the lived experience of artists and their communities.'[17] Such a formulation pinpoints conditions in a sense that evokes a number of debates on social engagement and usefulness in art since the 2010s. Specifically, it calls on the image of the 'useful museum', as trialled by, for example, MiMA in Middlesbrough, UK, where the arts institution was presented as a social infrastructure that is dedicated to supporting its communities in ways other than exhibiting and mediating art. The contradictions here come down, once again, to conditions. Access may be a preliminary to justice, just like visibility, but it remains a neutral descriptor, unless the power relations of the thing or experience to be accessed are part of the challenge.

However, the definition of access Lazard seems to be formulating is one that radically counters precisely the spectre of autoimmune personhood. This vision of self-enclosed, bounded and self-reliant individuals stands to be dismantled in favour of a more relational concept of people as subjects with needs and

16 Lazard, *Accessibility in the Arts*, 6.

17 Ibid., 9.

caring abilities as well as capacities and skills.[18] This then redefines labour as a relational and aesthetic activity rather than a productive and commodified one, and, once this relational element is front and centre, the contradictions of a predetermined visibility, usability, the unvarnished good of representation, start to diminish in importance. With them go the inclusivist and naturalising fantasies that form the hard barrier to this genre of radicalism.

Slices of operational autonomy

I have argued that Lazard and Leung both deal with the question of dependency – of conditions for (the) work to be made and be viewed – from a minimalist or post-conceptual starting point. It might be said that Leung works in a more reticent way in this territory, but the proximity is there. Atmosphere is a medium for her, with the barely noticed or proprioceptive as the range in which questions of access – to production time, to exhibition space – can be felt. Recent exhibitions such as *Balances* (Maxwell Graham, NYC, 2022) problematise access to an artistic identity, an artistic work schedule, in light of the gendered labour of parenthood. There is a chart explaining when the artist can work and when she cannot. There are baby monitors and child safety gates. Leung writes in the exhibition text that '[a] work is contingent on its context, this vulnerability is my work's resilience. It is a negotiation of what it means to have dependencies and be dependent. It is a negotiation of what it means to value the labour of maintenance.' Dependencies featured for Leung in the past as a formal principle 'below the radar', digging out the 'infra-thin' of

18 For more on the limits of the individual as a category, see Vishmidt, 'Bodies in Space: On the Limits of Vulnerability'.

an exhibition situation through colour, lighting and measurement. Yet, now, the dependency has ramified outside of that situation, extending to the question of what it takes to be personally present within the exhibition space in the first place.[19] This allows Leung to ask how such presence can be revised or enacted: presence itself becomes the basis for a series of works that self-reflexively pose the question of their own diagrammatic insufficiency – of their non-performativity as works or, rather, their performativity *as* the limits to working – in a denaturalising gesture already identified in the art of Ukeles. At the same time, Leung's insistence that her propositions are presented not only in space but as an analysis of spatial properties, as the core of what it means to make an exhibition, are *minimally* didactic, *minimally* present – an organisation of selected elements into a rebus or a rhyme of objects in a space that always has to do with atmosphere: a certain height of wall painted, a certain colour, a certain shape of light ornament, a certain sound coming from a certain fixture. The elements are never alone; they are always serial, the better to pattern the experience of the space. In this initially evident sense, Leung's approach is phenomenological as a tangent to the minimalist legacy, albeit less concerned with materiality or direct experience than with tweaking standard settings to tell stories and make jokes about dependency. A vanishing mediator, shedding an electric charge as it disappears around the wall at the corner of your eye.

But, even if spatiality has remained the focus for the artist, keeping the affect light and allegorical, the 2022 exhibition *Balances* started to extend the analysis into time: the recursive time of being available to think about art that entails a dependency somewhere else, through the hands and tools of others. The delegated performance of the install becomes the delegated

19 The 'infra-thin' is a concept coined, but not defined, by Marcel Duchamp, usually used to refer to nearly imperceptible differences.

performance of the reproductive and the waged labour that enables the artist to maintain their life and their family on the other side of the chain (one might even say the hierarchy of idea and execution), and the query becomes whether the *continuity* of these activities (be they thematised or hidden) can be visualised as the *absence* of time. So a space that is not just about modulating the visitor's experience as an allegory of dependency of art on standards, but also about going further back into the artist's production process as itself dependent on standards that cannot reasonably show up in the space of exhibition as anything but absences (sleep, exhaustion, caring tasks). Such a trajectory seems to merge with Lazard's exploration of the formal properties of access: all the ways the inaesthetic adaptation to 'special conditions' can be rerouted back into aesthetic conceptualisation. And this, perhaps, is what situates these two practices as belonging so intimately to the curatorial imagination of the exhibition *on affairs*, with its attention to how infrastructural thinking in post-conceptual artistic practice is capable of levering slices of operational autonomy out of a teeming image world where circulation and permutation never stops. As Peter Osborne has written, 'The photograph's "existential proximity to the world" – its indexicality – is thus increasingly registered less in the content of the image than in the often rapidly image-obliterating act of its exchange.'[20] His term 'distributive unity', denoting a fragile, historically bound way of unifying matter under a category (here, 'photography') always from a retrospectively unifying vantage, allows us to see that categories such as 'infrastructure', 'affairs' or even 'artwork' have no ontology to unify them except a historical one – that is, the possibility of understanding what we are referring to by

20 Quoting John Roberts, 'Photography after the Photograph: Event, Archive, and the Non-Symbolic', *Oxford Art Journal*, 32, 2 (2009), 283.

agreeing on what it is and how it works.[21] This baseline understanding of what we are looking at is identified in *on affairs* as a 'space of operations', of logistics and permutations.[22] Not a showcase of systems but of possible modes of experience mediated through materialisations that may include various levels of distributive unity, may include mathematical formulas, codes of conduct, may include temporality, gender, space, scent and texture. All resonate with an interest in dependency, on and off-site, structural and infrastructural.

Finally, in their refusal to accept naturalising shortcuts, both Lazard's and Leung's practices are compatible with a theoretical proposition: what if we use reproductive labour to analyse not how to feel better, but how to feel worse? Not as a thought experiment but as a form of collective practice. Reproduction should make us angry, because there's no reproduction outside the reproduction of the relations of production (the capital relation, in other words), the source of so much death, disability, exhaustion and exclusion. In spite of their marked differences – differences in form, period and also tone – the works of the artists considered in this chapter make it clear that there can be no 'care revolution' without much more fundamental forms of social transformation. Quoting the salient words of Jasmine Gibson in the journal of materialist feminism *LIES*, 'there will be no commoning but the commoning of our wrath and liberation'.[23]

21 Peter Osborne, *Anywhere or not at All: Philosophy of Contemporary Art*, London: Verso, 2013, Chapter 5.

22 Mezzadra and Neilson, *The Politics of Operations*.

23 Jasmine Gibson, 'The Fire This Time?', *LIES Journal*, 2 (2015), liesjournal.net.

5.
Entropy

Mining negativity

In the last chapter, we touched on the fact that reproductive work has always been experienced as a struggle against entropy. In Chantal Akerman's *Jeanne Dielman, 23 quai du Commerce, 1080 Bruxelles* (1975), we see the subjective effects of this outlined very clearly: entropy becomes a source of psychic terror and dis-organisation, which, in an effort to make sense of the senselessness, Akerman's protagonist tries to keep at bay with rules and routines, until she no longer can. In fact, entropy can be one of the key modalities through which we experience alienation from the manifest or unarguable 'usefulness' of reproductive labour: maintenance as 'unworking'. Here we might recall Akerman's first film, *Saute ma Ville* ('Blow Up My Town', 1968), which directly collides domestic maintenance, absurdity and self-abolition: cleaning the kitchen is just a prelude to blowing up the apartment block, blasting all the housewives out of their kitchens.

These two episodes from the reproductive history of entropy compel us to think about not just housework, even if women still do the majority of it, but the whole apparatus of gender that is thus thrown open. They're also a point of connection to the treatment of infrastructure, the conditions of social life, *as* reproductive. Just as the gender relation is denaturalised when gendered labour is depicted as something monstrous, abject but also prosaic and eccentric – with the domestic as a 'weird' or paradoxical space bereft of nature – entropy can allow for a different approach to the infrastructural altogether. Where, in a conventional usage, reproduction is permanent struggle against entropy, in a speculative register – already visible in Duchamp's or Ukeles's work – it can also become a collaboration with it, an entropic form, enabling the artist to make a cut in her own infrastructural conditions.

The current chapter will attempt to outline some related issues that I have been thinking about regarding art and energy, approached from the perspectives of infrastructure, value and labour. This will mean extending our discussion of infrastructure as conditions within the art field, a sort of 'transcendental' use of the concept, in the Kantian sense, to 'infrastructure' as it is more conventionally understood, as bridges, roads, telecoms and so on, as well as extractive infrastructure – the energy basis of present-day capitalist society. What we are trying to develop by this means is a critical approach to infrastructure as a kind of enabling constraint, an approach that involves moving between the synchronic diagram of infrastructure as a means of fixing or controlling time – this is how the geographer Timothy Mitchell understands the massive capital investments involved in large infrastructure projects – to the determinacies and contingencies of social relations as the content of historical materialism.[1]

Zooming out for a moment into the most abstract register of the category as I have been developing it, infrastructural critique is a reckoning with what it means that infrastructure persists and makes possible only insofar as it also makes impossible. As we argued in Chapter 1, infrastructure is always specific: it defines the material reproduction conditions of forms of social life and accumulation strategies that equate to destroyed life for some and wealth and comfort for others. This is the fundamental 'dialectic' of the extraction and waste disposal of labours, lives and natures, a further instantiation of the logic that runs throughout all of my

1 Timothy Mitchell, 'Infrastructures Work on Time'.

work of the constitutive status of the exception in relation to the rule.[2] In my understanding, there is a conceptual and strategic dimension to this focus, one of which is to counter visibility-based discourses of justice that are predicated on an ethics of recognition: it is not enough that the exception simply be recognised.

Entropy and exceptions intersect in the ways in which capitalist economies and societies operate, from the role of 'surplus value' in Marx to the role of 'cheap nature' in Jason W. Moore's analysis and that of other contemporary critical theories of capitalist society that focus on the 'exes-' of capital, beyond the long-recognised fundamentals of exchange and exploitation (extraction, expropriation . . .).[3] Political ecology shows us that the construction and devaluation of nature, from non-human life to 'naturalised' gendered and racialised labour, is a precondition of commodification: entropic waste is at once the exception to and constitutive of value. This process has been analysed in terms such as 'permanent primary (primitive) accumulation' or, latterly, 'accumulation by dispossession'.[4] It can likewise be found in the 'world-ecological surplus' discussed by Moore, which he uses to refer to the exhaustion of resources by the expansion of surplus

---

2 For more on this, see Vishmidt, *Speculation as a Mode of Production*, 142, 154; Marina Vishmidt, 'Externality and Necessity between Materialism and Ecology', in *Incomputable Earth*, edited by Antonia Majaca, London: Bloomsbury, 2026.

3 Jason W. Moore, *Capitalism in the Web of Life: Ecology and the Accumulation of Capital*, London: Verso, 2015, 23; Chris Chen and Sarika Chandra, 'Remapping the Race/Class Problematic', in *Totality Inside Out: Rethinking Crisis and Conflict under Capital*, edited by Kevin Floyd, Jen Hedler Phillis and Sarika Chandra, New York: Fordham University Press, 2022, 157.

4 The analysis of 'permanent primitive accumulation' is usually traced back to Rosa Luxemburg; for 'accumulation by dispossession' see David Harvey, *The New Imperialism*, Oxford: Oxford University Press, 2005.

capital.[5] This concept of the parallelism between capitalist production and waste in turn aligns with 'surplus population' identified by Marx as corollary with the capitalist mode of production, as well as the devaluation of reproductive labour discussed in the last chapter. Thus exhaustion, expulsion, extraction without reproduction (of labour power, of non-human life) is as key to the reproduction *of capital* as the reproduction of labour power, extending the contradiction identified by Marx between absorption and expulsion of labour power at the basis of his theory of the 'reserve army of labour'.[6] As has often been argued, every act of production by the worker is simultaneously the production of their own superfluity.[7] This dynamic has lately been revisited, if not always in the vocabulary of the critique of political economy, in projects looking at racialisation and the way it facilitates the 'surplusing' of specific communities. Mass incarceration and murderous policing represent the outcome of such surplusing in regimes of urban accumulation and the pushing of resource frontiers. Violence is the consequence, land expulsions, housing displacement, gentrification and the creation of 'sacrifice zones' the cause.[8]

---

5 Jason W. Moore, 'The End of Cheap Nature. Or How I Learned to Stop Worrying about "The" Environment and Love the Crisis of Capitalism', in *Structures of the World Political Economy and the Future of Global Conflict and Cooperation*, edited by Christian Suter and Christopher Chase Dunn, Münster: Lit Verlag, 2014.

6 Karl Marx, *Capital: A Critique of Political Economy, Volume I*, translated by Ben Fowkes, London: Penguin, 1992, 793.

7 Ibid. See also Marx's famous claim in the *Grundrisse* that 'capital is itself the moving contradiction'. See Karl Marx, *Grundrisse: Foundations of the Critique of Political Economy*, translated by Martin Nicolaus, Harmondsworth: Penguin, 706.

8 Endnotes, 'Misery and Debt: On the Logic and History of Surplus Populations and Surplus Capital', *Endnotes*, 2 (2010), endnotes.org.uk; Sherman, 'Infrastructures and the Ontological Question of Race'; Wilson

To put all of this more succinctly, we can say that value under capital is thus constituted through its exception – that which is without value or remains unaccounted for. In my view, this dynamic of inclusion and exclusion should be assessed from a strategic as well as a theoretical standpoint, to see how we can move away from 'accounting' paradigms in emancipatory politics more generally, whether in terms of socialist ecological transition or aesthetics and the art institution.[9] The problem is to link the concept of accounting to the question of representation. Entropy is the thematic of waste, the uncounted, the devalued, the invisible. The difficult task both in ecological struggles and the field of art is to move away from a perspective that simply affirms the exceptional or devalued, reinscribing recognition when the stakes are the identification, strategic or theoretical, of a key subject in the terrain of anti-capitalist critique or movements, be that on the basis of labour, gender, racialisation, sexuality or some other 'void of the situation', in Alain Badiou's terms.[10] But how to achieve this while, at the same time, refusing the shortcuts of an anti-identity politics position, which ends up affirming rather than negating something that should not be an identity category – class against all other relational and ascriptional identities?[11] This is perhaps the central problem to be kept in mind, as we discuss

Gilmore, *Golden Gulag*; Neferti Tadiar, *Remaindered Life*, Durham: Duke University Press, 2022.

9 Vishmidt, 'Externality and Necessity between Materialism and Ecology'; see also Beverley Best's important 'Wages for Housework Redux: Social Reproduction and the Utopian Dialectic of the Value-Form', *Theory and Event*, 24, 4 (2021).

10 Alain Badiou, *Ethics: An Essay on the Understanding of Evil*, translated by Peter Hallward, London: Verso, 2012, 57.

11 Vishmidt and Sutherland, '(Un)making Value', 70ff; for more on the stagnation of categories of struggle into administrative categories, see Vishmidt, 'Known Nowheres', 112.

some moments in art history in which entropy and energy have been the direct objects of analysis.

The nexus of infrastructural critique with entropic waste, geophysics and energy was, for me, initially prompted by the overwhelming media hype about non-fungible tokens (NFTs) in 2021 and 2022. I was already writing about these developments as the limit point of the climate nihilism of financialised capital when my thinking was reframed by an encounter with an essay by Elisabeth Nicula, in which she considered them in conjunction with some examples of canonical North American Land Art, as a way of producing waste, or voids.[12] This meant thinking NFTs as the ultimate artefacts of the economic primacy of extractivism – a theme already widely discussed – but also in dialogue with the colonial and patriarchal production of terrestrial voids such as deserts: the intimate nexus between the production of waste and the production of value. This in turn demonstrated how intense processes of property claims and capitalist abstraction also define both materially and formally the abstraction of land into art and the abstraction of URLs into crypto-collectibles, which, believe it or not, is, at the time of writing in late 2022, an ongoing market, albeit one a little less bouncy than it was.

Mining the void

Now, extraction and waste disposal are phenomena that have been prominent in recent ecological theory and criticism, even generating relatively new disciplines such as waste studies, and they have also been important synthetic categories that bring together the economic and social dimensions of profit-making,

12 Elisabeth Nicula, 'The Artist Is the Void', *Momus*, 10 May 2022.

value generation and disposability, from the extraction of resources in large-scale mining to the 'fracking' of attention and data in platform capitalist enterprises and the extraction of unpaid labour in social reproduction.[13] But, while I will get into these a little later, I would first like to think about how these categories of extraction and waste are mediated in geophysics, specifically through the concept of entropy. We are familiar with the basic idea of entropy as the tendency of any closed system to lose heat, energy, stability and organisation as time passes. It is the tendency of any energetic system to dissipate over time. A brief definition in the *Encyclopedia Britannica* puts it this way: 'entropy [is] the measure of a system's thermal energy per unit temperature that is unavailable for doing useful work. Because work is obtained from ordered molecular motion, the amount of entropy is also a measure of the molecular disorder, or randomness, of a system.'[14]

An even shorter definition is 'heat death' – an escalation of complexity, then a reversion into chaos, or 'de-differentiation', something that the contemporary acceleration of climate crisis seems to evoke very closely. In the context of thinking about Land Art and the production of voids, Nicula's piece comes close to describing this as the status of contemporary art as such. She writes, 'Sometimes I think I've forgotten what looking at art is for, and sometimes I think I never knew. In the case of the NFT makers, there's nothing to see at all, but there's a hole all the same.' Her wider argument, that Land Art and NFTs can be

---

13 Tadiar, *Remaindered Life*; Max Liboiron and Josh Lepawsky, *Discard Studies: Wasting, Systems, and Power*, Cambridge: MIT Press, 2022; Jathan Sadowski, 'When data is capital: Datafication, accumulation, and extraction', *Big Data and Society*, 6, 1 (2019): 1–12.

14 Gordon W. F. Drake, 'Entropy', *Encyclopedia Britannica*, britannica.com.

aligned on an axis of social perspective and economic/ecological dynamics, is also worth pursuing:

> Extraction – of natural resources and of labor – is the defining American act, at home and at war. Inasmuch as art is for the statement of itself, earthworks such as [Michael] Heizer's extract for the sake of extraction. To me he is the most patriotic of artists. The effect of an earthwork is never big enough to critique its circumstances nor generative enough to counter the harmful effects of its creation. In this, the NFT producers have accomplished something great, and outdone the 1970s land artists. With minimal labor, no pretense of theory or contextualization, no aesthetic clarity, and no object to speak of, they have set off exponential extractions. It's not new; it's just worse.[15]

Such an inquiry has to reckon from the start, of course, with the colonial imprint, conceptual and material, that the 'dematerialisation' heralded by Land Art in the 1960s and 1970s actually carried, especially when considering, as a lot of the writing on the newly finished Michael Heizer work *City* in the Nevada desert does, the neglect of or indifference to indigenous relationships to the land.[16] Dematerialisation was adopted as a strategy to escape an art market preoccupied with objects in order to focus on non-objects, non-sites and non-economies, but its conditions of possibility were US imperialism, industrial agriculture, Cold War military budgets and the displacement of indigenous communities that both provides resources and creates 'voids' for Land Artists to fill and formalise with their art. Or, as the contemporary US

15 Nicula, 'The Artist Is the Void'.

16 See Jasmine Liu, 'What Do Native Artists Think of Michael Heizer's New Land Art Work?', *Hyperallergic*, 21 September 2022.

indigenous-descent artist Alan Michelson put it a couple of years ago, in considering the relationship between his own use of the spiral motif and Smithson's *Spiral Jetty*, the practices of the canonical white male Land Art protagonists 'are ahistorical and despite a dystopian undercurrent, largely formal'.[17]

However, it might be worth drilling down, so to speak, from this accurate but rather general assessment. When it comes to his use of the category of 'entropy', one has the impression that Smithson sees his work as not so much glorifying or architecting the void as modelling the failure of human organisation of time and space through some strategic adjustments to the visible aspects of geologic time. This disposition shows some parallel with institutional critique. Smithson, whose 1972 essay 'Cultural Confinement' provided an acid diagnosis of the artist doing 'tough little tricks' in the gallery space, is a figure who in many ways anticipated the now burnt-out hopes of that cultural tendency. '[I]t would be better,' he wrote – anticipating a later argument of Andrea Fraser's – 'to disclose the confinement rather than make illusions of freedom.'[18]

Seen from another perspective, the rejection of institutionalisation is also a collaboration with entropy. Smithson wanted to study and somehow aesthetically clarify processes of disintegration. We can see him as a sort of lab technician of geological processes, hoping to realign them as windows into cultural ones, or memento mori for industrial civilisation. Not so much monuments to waste, then, as the juxtaposition between geologic process and acculturated notions of form and progress. For him, entropy is a geological, temporal and epistemological category,

17 Alan Michelson, interview in *After La vida nueva / Book of Gossip*, 2020.

18 Robert Smithson, 'Cultural Confinement', in *Collected Writings*, edited by Jack Flam, Berkeley: University of California Press, 1996, 155.

defining an approach that he suggests is adequate for comprehending and intervening in the immanent decay – the inherent vice or inbuilt limit – and chaotic senselessness of industrial civilisation. In this passage from an interview in 1971, titled, after a phrase in a Malcolm Lowry novel, 'The Earth, Subject to Cataclysms, is a Cruel Master', you can see him combine all the senses of entropy that were operative for him:

> Geology has its own kind of entropy, that has to do with sediment mixtures. Sediment plays a part in my work. Unlike Buckminster Fuller, I'm interested in collaborating with entropy. Someday I would like to compile all the different entropies. All the classifications would lose their grids. Levi-Strauss had a good insight; he suggested we change the study of anthropology into 'entropology'. It would be a study that devotes itself to the process of disintegration in highly developed structures. After all, wreckage is often more interesting than structure. At least, not as depressing as Dymaxion domes. Utopian saviors we can do without.[19]

Here, we might also want to think, with the philosopher Joel White, about the concept of 'entropic formness' – the idea that form can only persist under the constant threat of dissolution.[20] At the same time, we can see temporality in relation to geology as the constant shifting between presence and absence, the erosion of stability at the level of everyday experience just as entropy is the erosion – or condition – of stability at levels far away from

19 Smithson, 'The Earth, Subject to Cataclysms, Is a Cruel Master', *Collected Writings*, 256.

20 Joel White, 'Analogy of a Dying Star: Entropic Formness', *Pli: Warwick Journal of Philosophy*, 32 (2020).

perception, like the molecular and the cosmic. Here, I recently found the Apple TV+ production *Prehistoric Planet* a weirdly helpful way to think about this, a CGI 'documentary' that purports to have been made in prehistoric time and which narrates an irreversible trajectory towards extinction – a kind of novel, mass cultural 'entropology'. We may also recall that time is the condition for the infrastructural 'cuts' discussed in Chapter 3, the points where institutions break down and the infrastructure comes momentarily into view, as resource and basis for practical intervention.

A radically simplified version of this entropic trajectory is at work in the compelling rhythm that can be detected in Nicula's analysis, between the production of voids in a desert landscape via Land Art such as Michael Heizer's *Double Negative* and the profligate burning of energy that generates cryptocurrencies in general and NFTs in particular. You could almost link them both to the aesthetic as 'purposeless purpose' in Kant, or his analysis of the 'sublime' as a phenomenon 'out there', generally in nature, that overwhelms us with contradictory feelings of our physical limits and moral infinity. Nicula puts it well when she speaks about the NFT producers 'outdoing' land artists. Here she marks a very intriguing conjuncture that is, at the same time, somewhat familiar from Western aesthetic philosophy: between the sublime and the nihilistic.[21] The point corresponds with a current of thinking that has lately played a part in the aesthetic critique of financialised capitalism, as well as its extractive face in the numerous visual records, made by drone and by hand, of the moonscapes of capitalist extraction: of 'sacrifice zones' of mining and

21 See, for example, Jean-Francois Lyotard, 'An Answer to the Question, What is the Postmodern?', in *The Postmodern Explained: Correspondence, 1982–85*, translated by Julian Pefanis et al., Minneapolis: University of Minnesota Press, 1993, 19.

pollution in the US, South America, China and elsewhere. Whether these records are made by contemporary artists or documentary filmmakers, this mode of representation is now and has been for some time a contemporary cliché, in the same genre as the 'Great Pacific Garbage Patch' of plastic, for example. In any case, what Nicula succeeds in doing, in a very condensed and pointed way, is to underline the sheer banality of this kind of sublime, its aesthetic deficit, and how the established infrastructure of extraction, waste and domination subtends the new and shiny, 'decentralised' and 'disintermediated' world of the NFT. As she says, where exactly did that 240,000 'irrelevant' tons of sandstone Heizer displaced for the creation of *Double Negative* go?

Non-identical infrastructure

So where does that leave us, in light of the foregoing attempts to parse the intricate and often twisted relations between the politics of visibility, which strives to render an account and thus go some way towards normalisation, and the structural centrality of the exception to capitalist valorisation? I would now like to turn from the production of voids to the fabric of plenitude, in order to suggest a different vocabulary for thinking the dynamics of visibility than the one drawn from capitalist accounting logics. The connection can be made speculatively, in terms of the recognition of what is already there but (infra)structurally disregarded in capitalism, whether this be building materials or labour. I am particularly interested here in the relation of two apparently quite distinct tendencies, namely the principles of circular economy when it comes to construction, on the one hand, and of unionisation when it comes to labour, on the other. 'Circular' economy, the idea of a form of economics focused on reuse and sustainability, is of course by now one of the main ecological propositions in all kinds of journalistic, theoretical and policy contexts, and treated in isolation can take on the character of a feel-good regulative ideal. But can we approach it differently, as a way of bridging the two sides of a recognition-based rebalancing of an economy, its technical and political composition?

My proposition, in other words, is to treat circular economy as an anti-entropy principle – a means of *organising* – while asking what a processual category such as recycling has to do with the idea of a solid, timeless one such as infrastructure. Does it, paradoxically, introduce a kind of entropy into that idea? Could it invert the relation of domination captured by Timothy Mitchell in the title of his essay 'Infrastructures Work on Time', and allow time 'to work' on infrastructure instead? In posing these questions, I am thinking about the kinds of activities outlined in architect Lindsey Wikstrom's essay 'A Gold Mine, Above Ground', where she contends that extractivism can be neutralised, materially, economically and societally by simply mining materials, including materials for energy infrastructure such as electric batteries and solar panels, from existing buildings rather than from the earth or the seafloor. Treating buildings as 'above-ground' mines can act as an alternative to demolishing them and feeding a wasteful economy of supposedly environmentally responsible new architecture. As Wikstrom writes:

> Like smartphones, entire buildings are also being buried with their valuables inside. The volume of waste produced by building materials far surpasses the volume of all other waste [. . .] Recovering materials through mechanical and chemical processes is an urgently needed form of infrastructure. To utilise above-ground building materials in this way, new economies and technology are needed to make the above-ground stock legible and deployable. Similar to geologists and foresters who help locate mines or plan tree

> farms, as well as tracking their changes over time, there will soon arise experts who can read the landscape of above-ground building materials and navigate the data to utilize it for anthropological and ecological gain. Detailed knowledge about embedded materials in buildings, their characteristics and chemistry, are crucial for accessing this gold mine above ground.[22]

In a speculative register, I would suggest that what we see here is a variation on the politics of recognition or visibility more often encountered in the domain of social justice, here premised on seeing what is already there as an essential part of building something new.[23]

But we can push this speculative connection further. In recent years, architects in the US have been coming together to build their own power as workers, initiating organisations that attempt to recognise a previously disregarded commonality between their own work and that of wage labourers of other kinds. The manifesto of The Architecture Lobby connects this activity to the demand that climate justice become 'the basis of all architectural work'.[24] So, here, two types of 'politics of recognition' intersect, and similar developments can be seen in many other capitalist countries. In 2022, during a major escalation of strike activity both in the private and public sectors triggered by increases in the costs of living, architects in London formed a new branch of the United Voices of the World, a grassroots union that has been

22 Lindsey Wikstrom, 'A Gold Mine, Above Ground', *e-flux*, September 2022, e-flux.com.

23 At the same time, Wikstrom's argument questions 'efficiency' as the hallmark of material use – an unusual move, since efficiency is often smuggled into even ecological discussion without attending to the capitalist, or certainly instrumental, frameworks it implies.

24 See the 'About' page on architecture-lobby.org.

involved with the organisation of low-paid and migrant workers, and which recently has expanded to include workers who had until recently not thought of themselves in these terms, such as graphic designers and cultural workers.[25] My suggestion is that the politics of visibility emerging here is a type of practical critique that aims to transform a field, or its infrastructure, by collapsing and discrediting one set of norms and proposing another, in a process that cuts new channels between the technical and the social, the material and the political. Coming back to an argument that we made at the beginning of Chapter 1, we can say that this is a way of thinking identity speculatively, through the antagonistic unity of sameness and difference.

The most compelling philosophical language for thinking this approach is found in the work of Adorno. Earlier, I mentioned his thinking around 'non-identity' – his idea that 'objects do not go into their concepts without leaving a remainder, that they come to contradict the traditional norm of adequacy'.[26] Non-identity, in this sense, serves as an approach to the politics of recognition based in the speculative and going beyond the usual gestures of inclusion, making visible ('identifying') in order to articulate a practical relation to an existing norm. When Adorno spoke of 'norm[s] of adequacy', he meant traditional epistemic norms, though of course in his work the word was already laden with social and political connotations. He argued that, because

25 See the 'About' page on uvw-saw.org.uk. The union began by organising with cleaners and security guards, mostly of a migrant background, so its decision to organise workers not typically considered to be 'class conscious' can itself be considered a transversal move. For more on the unionisation of previously unorganised sectors, see Jamie Woodcock, *Marx at the Arcade: Consoles, Controllers, and Class Struggle*, Chicago: Haymarket, 2019. Additional coverage and analysis can be found in the journal *Notes from Below*.

26 Adorno, *Negative Dialectics*, 143ff.

thinking is a striving for definition, it seeks to unify the heterogeneous (creating an identity); yet by trying to break through the logical agreement thought creates between its objects and the concepts it uses to comprehend them, you end up with contradiction. This is a 'legal' concept, insofar as it is defined within the so-called laws of classical Western logic, such as the law of the excluded middle. A familiar version of this states that, if we take a proposition *P*, 'Socrates is mortal', then the statement must be either true or false. It is logically untenable that *P* is both. Something must be objectively true *or* false, it cannot be 'different', or fall out of the rules of logic, or obey a different logical system. What Adorno is saying is that this legal orientation of the structure of Western thought means that it is also a law that stabilises difference in order to make it legible within its system.[27] Contradiction can become just another principle to uphold identity, the supposed adequacy between conceptual thought and material reality: 'contradiction is non-identity under the aspect of identity; the dialectical primacy of the principle of contradiction makes the thought of unity the measure of heterogeneity'.[28] This argument remains the case unless dialectics is consistently pursued – which is exactly what is meant by the 'negativity' Adorno is concerned to develop for dialectical thinking. Despite the limits and lapses in Hegel's work, we can say internal differentiation rather than positivity is the motor of his speculative dialectics as well, which is why its capacity for revealing and registering antagonism was compelling for Marx's own use of dialectics in his social theory.[29]

27 On 'law' in this wider sense, see Brenna Bhandar, *The Colonial Lives of Property: Law, Land, and Racial Regimes of Ownership*, Durham: Duke University Press, 2018.

28 Adorno, *Negative Dialectics*, 5.

29 *Speculation as a Mode of Production*, 9, 82–3.

In relation to entropy, we could say that a perspective that takes entropy into account is one that sees transformability as a capacity of entropy, one that has to be realised socially and politically, rather than aestheticised as a natural process in the poetic, conceptually precise but ultimately insular way we can see in Smithson's work. He sees entropy rather than progress in industrial civilisation, but entropy without a perspective of transformation looks a lot like atrophy, which brings us back to Nicula's pairing of canonical examples from Land Art with NFTs.

In light of this, I am suggesting that we see the political implications of projects such as circular economy and independent trade union organisation as ways of articulating the method of non-identity. They do this insofar as part of their constitutive process is a recontextualisation, a new recognition or a disclosure of difference, where a positive, established, unquestioned norm, process or institution once stood. The norm reproduced a set of unjust and indefensible practices from a social or an ecological perspective, while the counter-practices articulate both a difference (an imbalance or injustice) that was suppressed within these practices while also enabling them to operate, *and* a different relation between the social and ecological – the basis of a new political proposition. Thus, I would suggest that we do not set up an opposition between a politics of visibility and a politics of opacity or refusal, but instead work in the mode of both/and, the transformative and constitutive. In looking to the conceptual resources of non-identity thinking in our praxis, which moves through but also beyond contradiction, we are forced constantly to redraw and restrategise our critical categories not just in light of experience, but in terms of what kind of transformation we are moving towards – and, perhaps, against.

Finally, this also brings us to a question central to institutional critique, about the use of 'the boundary between outside and inside' by movements that are transversal to the grammar and institution of art. It raises the question of the institution's operation of 'bringing in' and 'keeping out', which is more or less the only ontology of art that we can still find credible. Further, it poses the question of how that mode of critical 'laundering', the accumulation and centrifuging of social phenomena, contradictions and histories as artistic and curatorial material, emerges as a key resource. Does there have to be a sort of transformation of cultural capital into waste before it becomes a political process, a kind of reverse engineering of the sedimentation of content into form that the institution performs? And could there be a pedagogical aspect to this desedimentation? Is the evacuation of context, the displacement of social praxis, performed by the production and display of contemporary art, an educational and thereby potentially a speculative process, as it is, for example, in the work of Mierle Laderman Ukeles, in which the displacement of housework becomes a speculative means of critique, both of housework and art? Across all of these questions, I am interested in the accumulation of waste product as art, on the one hand, and the repurposing of art as waste for a political process – its determinate negation – on the other. Entropy is another way of refractively using the power of the boundary between inside and outside that institutions uphold in the pursuit of ends other than institutional reproduction.

6. Abolition

[D]esire is part of the infrastructure.

Deleuze and Guattari, *Anti-Oedipus*

If we had been in the hold and were never held, we were never, neither, actually excluded by 'the black letter of the law', which all along wrote something like the depression of our inclusion as the color line; black subjectivity is the horrible harmony of power and intimacy.

Simone White, *Dear Angel of Death*

For more than a decade, Cameron Rowland has been engaged in making something like a museum of racial capitalism minus costumed re-enactors and plus a remarkable and ever more attuned grasp of how to mediate webs of real abstraction in art institutional space. 'Museum' is perhaps inapt, as 'continuing violations' are the fabric of its historiography; the format of a visitor centre is closer to the matter, its artefacts purposefully excerpted from daily use to demonstrate something, or offer a manual. What is salient about this work, however, is not just the acuity with which it depicts or the totality of what is disclosed in the research apparatus. It's the actual boring into the legal infrastructures of property that has marked Rowland's project over the span of its iterations. If property survives its abolition, as in the case of chattel slavery, and even thrives – as in the globalised free-trade boom experienced by Britain in the wake of the 1833 Abolition Act cited in the title of their Institute of Contemporary

Art (ICA) show in London, *3 & 4 Will. IV c. 73* – then, like all capitalist relationships, it is racked by antagonism, and the contradictions of its life can always be dramatically, diagrammatically, pushed, which is what Rowland does.

In this final chapter, we will try to establish some terms of infrastructural analysis that might help us to apprehend the stakes of this work, its 360-degree treatment of material experience and legal abstraction and the histories it pursues into the present. At the theoretical level, I will articulate some of the ways in which negativity and the related, totalising framework of (self-)abolition have developed in my thinking, before returning to the specific conjunction of the afterlives of chattel slavery, abolition and infrastructure in contemporary Black studies in general, and Rowland's work in particular. If, as this book has argued from the beginning, attention to infrastructure is at its core a way to try to develop a materialist theory of 'conditions', as enabling constraints, then it should be a way of reckoning with social abstraction, including the activity of finance, as a condition of possibility and impossibility. Rowland's work allows us to see this conjunction of the abstract and material in ways that are painfully fine-grained.[1]

It also helps us to think negation, and here we can introduce the idea of a kind of 'burdened materialism'. In this, I am thinking of the historian Saidiya Hartman's discussion of 'burdened individuality' as one key parameter of the afterlife of chattel slavery in North America – that is, the paradoxical or double-bind configuration of the imperative on the formally emancipated Black person to be a free liberal subject in a white supremacist society.[2] A 'burdened materialism' would then be a critical approach that moves between speculative form and empirical realism by working with and on real-world infrastructures, seen both as models

1 Peter Osborne, *Anywhere or Not at All*, 10.

2 Saidiya Hartman, *Scenes of Subjection*, Chapter 4.

and devices of making possible and impossible the circulation of value. What makes this approach 'burdened'? In my view, it is its exploitation of the formalisms and abstractions of these infrastructures to both show and effectively thwart the ways in which they reproduce dysfunction, inequality, profit, death, refusing to treat infrastructure independently of its social and historical presuppositions, even while making use of it. The role of blockage in Rowland's work and, in particular, the work's strategic conversion of assets *into* burdens enacts such a transformation of the relationship between people, state and materiality, relating to abolition as a generative as well as a 'destituting' tactic.[3]

From criticality to tear gas

If we acknowledge that art – as practice and as institution – is multiply mediated, we see that it constitutes a mediation in its own right, a function to which its status as exception is decisive. In modernity, art has represented a safe space for eternal human values, a means of class mobility, and finally a mystified last resort of freedom, a sphere of licensed dissent whose incursions into political visibility or celebrity culture serve as a foil to the more abiding facts of insulation and isolation. Art has held on to a utopian character precisely due to this insulation, even as it has been increasingly called upon to serve as an institutional redoubt for forms of cultural and political opposition that have been

3 Lucy Pia, 'Source Materials: Discursive Aspects in Cameron Rowland's Art', *FKW // Zeitschrift für Geschlechterforschung und Visuelle Kultur*, 73 (January 2024); Saidiya Hartman, Christina Sharpe, Rinaldo Walcott and Vicky Osterweil, *Diversity of Aesthetics*, vol. 3, *Looting*, edited by Andreas Petrossiants and Jose Rosales, New York: Emily Harvey Foundation; Andreas Petrossiants, 'Preliminary Notes Towards a Destituent Art', *Social Text*, 42, 2 (2024).

crowded out of their older, welfare capitalist social spaces and channels. And, yet, in an age where capitalist extraction seems increasingly less in need of mediations that can legitimate its rule – mediations such as culture, education or even formal, much less substantive, democracy – art also tends ever more relentlessly to become a status good, less distinct from other types of luxury commodities and investment sectors. Hence, the role of criticality in artistic discourse, functioning as it has in recent years as the marker of conflicted empathy with the victims of unchangeable social conditions, becomes increasingly superfluous, and thereby inflationary, in line with the production it concerns itself with. And yet despite or perhaps because of this, a 'turn' may be observed, in which art institutions of all types rush to match their shrinking budgets with more radical content that makes a 'second appearance', now as pedagogy or gesture, in the space of cultural production. Here, cachet is drawn from the academy or grassroots activity that may have developed elsewhere or in another historical moment, while in return a platform is offered – one that is hard to jettison, for strategic no less than economic reasons.

Art's distance from the strictures of the economy on a daily, experiential basis is important and critically productive, but also, invariably, ambiguous. It is only when this anomaly is connected to the reproduction of the anomalous as the geophysical and social crises manifesting everywhere – the 'expulsions', as Saskia Sassen calls it, and extractions of the current mode of valorisation, no less than the violent condensations of ethnic and gender supremacy that such 'endo-colonising' ways of valorisation entail – that exceptionality can develop political traction.[4] The fetishism

4 Saskia Sassen, *Expulsions: Brutality and Complexity in the Global Economy*, Cambridge: Harvard University Press, 2014. On 'endo-colonising' tendencies, see Rosa Luxemburg, *The Accumulation*

of the free individual and the independence of the juridical sphere correlate to one another, both underpinned by the fetishism of the commodity as the effective premise of all legal institutions in their fundamental commitment to the defence of private property. Here, the commodity itself can be seen as an infrastructure or a 'social form', in the tradition of Marxist value-form theory, rather than as a carrier of the 'satisfaction of needs' in a sphere of economic exchange driven by a naturalised feedback of supply and demand.[5] Likewise the social and the economic are, in their separation, ideological outcomes of a capitalist infrastructure – a mode of social production and reproduction – that operates through crisis and contradiction, which is to say, by means of yet more anomalies and exceptions. In this light, the economic exceptionality of art as non-value-productive aligns with other 'exceptions' and 'externalities' that lend themselves to an anti-capitalist reading not by means of their structural exceptionality but by their potential for antagonism. Or, in other words, what we could discuss as the actualisation of exceptionality – what I have elsewhere called an 'activated negativity'.[6]

---

of Capital, London: Routledge, 2003; Silvia Federici, *Caliban and the Witch: Women, the Body and Primitive Accumulation*, New York: Autonomedia; Maria Mies, *Patriarchy and Accumulation on a World Scale: Women in the International Division of Labour*, London: Zed Books, 2022.

5 For Marxist value-form theory, see the Introduction to *Marxism and the Critique of Value*, edited by Neil Larsen, Mathias Nilges, Josh Robinson and Nicholas Brown, Chicago: M-C-M', 2014, mcmprime.com; Patrick Murray, *The Mismeasure of Wealth: Essays on Marx and Social Form*, Leiden: Brill, 2016; Best, 'Wages for Housework Redux'.

6 Dave Beech, *Art and Value: Art's Economic Exceptionalism in Classical, Neoclassical and Marxist Economics*, Leiden: Brill, 2015; Julia Calver, Mira Mattar and Marina Vishmidt, 'Activated Negativity: An Interview with Marina Vishmidt', *Makhzin*, 2 (2016), makhzin.org.

What does this mean for art and infrastructural critique? Throughout this book, we have been arguing that capitalist value relations are constituted through their outsides and exceptions. Waste, abjection, the non-value of art, the entropy of environmental decay, non-valued or non-waged labour, extracted material resources and the burdened subjectivity of the slave are all distinct 'outsides' for capital on which capital nevertheless relies. At the same time, we have been arguing that it is not sufficient simply to attempt a 'revaluation of values'. Efforts to create a moral economy around that which 'does not count' overlook the ways in which what counts and what doesn't are dialectically interrelated under capital, as part of a negative totality. Affirmation of the exception proves, in the end, to be indirect affirmation of the rule. Our approach has, rather, been to argue that actually existing artistic autonomy lies instead in its capacity to act in and as determinate negation. As the philosopher Iain McDonald has written, this Hegelian idea refers to a point 'whereby consciousness experiences contradiction not as something meaningless or aporetic, but rather as the negative force that propels it to determine (to think through and diagnose, in other words) contradictions in order to overcome them or "negate" them'.[7]

But 'determinate negation' in contemporary art is rare if not impossible. In art fairs, biennials and gallery exhibitions, determinacy is more frequently encountered in the guise of affirmation – that is to say, as the identification and implementation of concrete if acupunctural goals of social use-value that are furthered via the techniques and resources of the institution of art and, perhaps more broadly, the 'culture industry', depending on the policy guiding the project. These then entail strategic reroutings of the social and economic value ('social capital') generated in the institution

7 Iain McDonald, 'Cold, Cold, Warm: Autonomy, intimacy and maturity in Adorno', *Philosophy and Social Criticism*, 37 (2011).

of art for ends located elsewhere, in a win-win scenario for the artist, the 'community', the art public and other entities, such as diplomats, NGOs and real-estate developers. We can think here of figures such as Theaster Gates and his dual economy of institutional art success and neighbourhood revitalisation, Renzo Martens and his dual economy of Western art institutional success and rural Congolese cultural and economic development or Marjetica Potrč and her small-scale environmental projects that traverse specific locations and the global art circuit.[8]

In searching for a negative current in contemporary art, we might begin with incidents such as the call to remove and destroy Dana Schutz's painting of a press photograph of Emmett Till in his coffin, included in the 2017 Whitney Biennial. These throw a stark light on the uneasy dialectic between the critical theory account of negation-as-autonomy and a more volatile stance of negation-as-struggle that can form the parameters for political action in the artistic sphere, particularly attending to the radical cancellation (rather than expansion) of 'the world' enunciated in 'afro-pessimist' thinking.[9] I would also suggest that contemporary politics of institutional negation such as boycotts have relevant strategic objectives, such as challenging the composition of museum boards and the role of private philanthropy in cultural support, or delegitimating hydrocarbon majors as suitable museum patrons in the case of

---

8 See Marina Vishmidt, 'Mimesis of the Hardened and Alienated', *e-flux* (March 2013), e-flux.com; 'Pure Maintenance', *South as a State of Mind* (2018), southasastateofmind.com. And for a more complex case, Marina Vishmidt, 'Nothing to See Here: On the Bracketing of the Spectator in a Hyperrelational Exhibition', *Grey Room*, 92 (Summer 2023).

9 Alex Greenberger, '"The Painting Must Go": Hannah Black Pens Open Letter to the Whitney About Controversial Biennial Work', *ArtNews*, 21 March 2017, artnews.com.

Tate or the British Museum. For example, two years after the call to destroy Schutz's painting, an article by Hannah Black, Ciarán Finlayson and Tobi Haslett in *Artforum* called for a boycott of the Whitney Biennial in order to build pressure for the removal of Warren Kanders from the board of the Whitney, due to his involvement, as CEO of Safariland, in selling military equipment and tear gas to US law enforcement and repressive states worldwide.[10]

Alongside the short-term objectives that can be achieved, such as getting a few cultural institutions to delink from BP, or making the Sacklers personae non gratae in the Anglophone funding landscape, the achievement of medium-term or long-term objectives succeeds insofar as these campaigns escape the frame of art politics and act in coalition with other social movements – the Warren Kanders situation, for example, was always about the structure of museum boards and not just about Kanders himself, and we can see that the main agents here were not the artists but the Whitney museum workers who first raised the issue and the many groups organising around police violence, migration and gentrification/displacement, such as Decolonize This Place.

From this very cursory overview, we can thus see that the performativity, or, rather, the praxis, of negation has the capacity to suspend the overdetermined space of who can perform as a critical subject or an aesthetic subject by taking on the contingent effects (emotional and political) and burdensome affects of working in solidarity, rather than affirming a fantasy of 'rationality' as authentic criticality. At the same time, the

10 Hannah Black, Tobi Haslett and Ciarán Finlayson, 'The Tear Gas Biennial', *Art Forum*, artforum.com. In 2023, *Artforum* was boycotted in turn, after the publication of an open letter denouncing the war on Gaza led to the firing of its editor-in-chief David Velasco.

performative totalisation of demands for abolition has the potential to make the mediations essential to an infrastructural critique – what I referred to in the last paragraph as strategic or medium-term goals – impossible to hold in view. On the one hand, practices of negation that risk the conditions of possibility of their own inscription into the excluding spaces of the cultural, aesthetic and academic can create an impetus to build long-term and liveable structures on other principles. On the other hand, discourses of negation also have the potential to shore up the institution, by advancing the proliferation of conceptual commodities, the more performatively radical the better. The important examples just cited show us that this is an issue not just of either/or, but of pitching critique at an infrastructural (enabling and extending) rather than an institutional (preserving and legitimating) level. It is from the specific articulation of this critique, perhaps, that there can emerge a speculative identity between the practice of infrastructural critique and the political horizon of abolition – the moment when the exception negates the rule.

A collective desire for a concrete something else

When I was first installed in an academic post, I experienced something I had managed to avoid for a long time. This was the experience of being attached and subordinated to 'iron cages' of administrative irrationality, without being precisely able to detect which modular component of the whole installation was the wrong, the diseased, the intractable one. It was all intractable, as each system mediated the others, and each was animated by its human components' attempts to further mediate it among one another, various strata of the academic population, and wield it in a way that is as analgesic as possible for each of the persons involved. I taught a course that was divided between a critical and a policy outlook, on which even to so much as pose the question of self-abolition would have been very difficult – a question of mobilising a collective body in which each identifies with each, each identifies themselves with the institution, but, ultimately, wants to go home at the end of the day, with these ties remaining elastic. Such as we are, we can only experience the command to scrutinise the conditions of our labour as a crisis, as a blow from the outside. Undertaking to methodically dismantle them is something only those who have power over our lives could be expected to do, and we are not among those people. Our subjugation is reproduced by the inability to pinpoint what's wrong, where the identification comes into view or into question, and in the giant concatenation of systems that constitute the site of our alienated and, perhaps, thematically challenging, 'interesting' labour. New to such a vortex still, I found it impossible to maintain any equilibrium in it, and every day by 3 p.m. I felt psychically destroyed, unable to dissociate or to remember what it was I was supposed to be doing, even while recognising my share in the machine-feeding schedule was a relatively light one, really almost imperceptible.

Amid the confessional perplexity here, I hope to have indicated something at least, namely the liminality of the concept of self-abolition – whether of class, gender or race – inasmuch as it talks about or imagines a negativity that is not refusal, not withdrawal, but that goes beyond them as a collective composition of withdrawals, a strike against one's place in the relation of reproduction or a counter-reproductive labour.[11] It is collective because

11 See Marina Vishmidt, 'Counter (Re)Productive Labour', *Autoitalia South East*, 4 April 2012, autoitaliasoutheast.org; *Speculation as a Mode of Production*, 92, 116; Christopher J. Arthur, *The New Dialectic and Marx's* Capital, Leiden: Brill, 2004, 54.

it is a kind of institutional critique; it attacks from within the desire and ability to maintain a state of normality, or normativity, in the service of a larger project of justice, understood as a collective creation of another means of living collectively. It is violent; in different ways, perhaps it is just abrupt. It is a concept that I first began to think in relation to its Marxist variant, the self-abolition of the proletariat, before studying its role in feminist and anti-racist movements, and, in each case, I want to highlight the dimension of collective and creative self-activity in the act of negation – self-abolition as self-determination – and that of biopower, the reproduction of docile and productive bodies in naturalised relations of exploitation and domination that often take on the contractual self-evidence of freedom, objectivity and justice.[12] It is, also, an injunction – think of the famous directive from some late 1970s Milanese feminist groups: 'In the meantime, destroy the bosses that are in you, destroy the capitalistic characteristics within you, destroy yourselves as our bosses, destroy yourselves as the inexhaustible vacuums of our domestic labour.'[13] This command is addressed foremost to male comrades – that is, to those who already recognise the necessity of broad social transformation. Those who would be free need to consider whose subjugation their freedom presupposes: as the trenchant phrase from Pierre Macherey has it, most juridical relationships conceal a relationship that is not itself juridical – an insight that has become increasingly central to contemporary radical feminist and Black radical discourse, from Carole Pateman to Angela Mitropoulos to Fred Moten to Hannah Black, who has written

12 In relation to biopolitics, see Claire Fontaine, *Human Strike Has Already Begun*.

13 'Several Milanese Feminist Groups', 'Destroy yourselves as our bosses. Destroy yourselves as the inexhaustible vacuums of our domestic labor', *New Inquiry*, 21 May (2012), thenewinquiry.com.

about the subject and abstraction in terms of how 'freedom isn't free'.[14]

Thus we come to the problematic of self-abolition by those who have neither selves nor labour to organise around, those who do not have access to the freedom to imagine otherwise. But this is not quite true. Prisoners organise and go on strike. So do those who do non-market-mediated work at home, and market-mediated sex work. Social abjection does not always have to wait for the theorist, sociologist, activist or artist to valorise it. It can be a shared condition of negativity in the sense of the negativity *that is already there*, in the conditions, as the incipient refusal within obedience, production and reproduction. Here, I would like to point to a very insightful recent discussion by the feminist poet Amy De'Ath, who takes the notion of the 'abject' both from Julia Kristeva and *Endnotes* in their text 'Logic of Gender', where it defines the kind of labour that is too devalued to be subsumed into the market, but is still predominantly enforced, conventionally or violently, with violence as the delivery vehicle of convention. 'It is hard,' De'Ath writes, 'to make the abject, the "dealing with", visible to those who do not have to do it. It is hard or impossible to make these things visible, let alone understood in representational or economic terms.'[15] I think we can probably unpick the ways in which this 'dealing with' has come to unfold politically, across many inter-mediated and cross-contaminated scales of

---

14 Pierre Macherey, 'The Productive Subject', *Viewpoint Magazine*, 31 May 2015, viewpointmag.com; Carole Pateman, *The Sexual Contract*, Stanford: Stanford University Press, 1988; Angela Mitropoulos, *Contract and Contagion: From Biopolitics to Oikonomia*, Wivenhoe: Minor Compositions, 2012; Fred Moten, 'Jurisgenerative Grammar (for alto)', in *Oxford Handbook of Critical Improvisation Studies*, edited by George Lewis, Oxford: Oxford University Press, 2016; Hannah Black, 'Fractal Freedoms', *Afterall: A Journal of Art, Context and Enquiry*, 41 (Spring/Summer 2016).

15 Amy De'Ath, 'L(a)ying Down in the Banlieue', *Mute*, 21 September 2016, metamute.org.

gendered and racialised visibility. Abjection's relation to self-abolition might mean that what has been abjected drives the commitment to abolish as in not to be 'that', as part of the project to expand and complicate social experience. That which cannot be subsumed because it is not worth subsuming – into labour, into government, into speech – must somehow be understood as the libidinal impetus to an abolition that is neither juridical nor volitional but a realisation of the unthought as collective power, just as it is the unthought that reproduces collective humiliation, beyond even the devices of narcissistic self-narration.[16] By this, I mean self-abolition can have an abstract valence to it. It sounds as if it can be a decision, a proclamation, like the abolition of slavery for example. I am searching for a materialist and not a gestural resonance for this concept, and, so far, the main parameter I've found is that it has to be collective – a collective desire for a concrete something else. But even this is not satisfying. Again, the problem for infrastructural critique is to avoid the fetishisation of negation as property of a deciding subject, or as a dissolution of the subject into undifferentiated life – a 'paradox' of self-abolition thematised in an important essay by the philosopher Ray Brassier.[17]

Tearing up the civil contract

In our current situation, the richest theorisation of this 'deciding subject' has emerged from the field of contemporary Black studies. The racialisation of those social subjects exposed to

16 The phrase 'the position of the unthought' comes from a discussion between Saidiya Hartman and Frank Wilderson, 'The Position of the Unthought', *Qui Parle*, 13, 2 (Spring/Summer 2003).

17 Ray Brassier, 'Wandering Abstraction', *Mute*, 13 February 2014, metamute.org.

'exceptional' levels of violence, control and subjugation, whether as labour power or as social surplus, is the anomaly that founds the norm of autonomous critical-aesthetic personhood. To engage this subject without analysing dispossession and dehumanisation – including through the work of those scholars who give us the tools to understand what kind of thing (or relation) modernity, or modern art, *is*, such as Fred Moten, Denise Ferreira da Silva, Brenna Bhandar, David Lloyd or Saidiya Hartman – is not so much an omission as a way of producing the wrong structure of thought altogether. To take one example, David Lloyd's *Under Representation*, a collection of essays that marks a decades-long engagement with the Western philosophical aesthetics canon, especially Kant and Hegel, constructs a layered argument about how the very forms of normativity promulgated by such philosophical aesthetics, with their visions of educated sensibility and the 'civil contract' of the cultural, both disavow and naturalise how the racialised and colonial taxonomies of modernity saturate their construction of the subject of aesthetic judgement.[18]

Two decades of this increasingly visible and trenchant work allows us to contrast another approach to negation that does not renounce the perspective of abolition, but which begins from the recognition that 'there was [not] a radical enough break to reposition the black body after Jubilee'.[19] To the Hegel-inspired ontology of art as sensuous non-identity, it counters with a different version of totality – the ontology of Black abjection as it is both expelled from and constitutive of non-Black social life or 'civil society' in general. An important distinction Frank B. Wilderson III makes

18 Lloyd, *Under Representation*; on the 'civil contract', see Ariella Azoulay, *The Civil Contract of Photography*, translated by Rela Mazali and Ruvik Danieli, Princeton: Princeton University Press, 2012.

19 Hartman and Wilderson, 'Position of the Unthought', 183. Wilderson is here describing a central argument of Hartman's *Scenes of Subjection*.

between 'trying to build a better world' and the Black opposition to such a project can be traced, as Lloyd's work confirms from a different perspective, back to Kant's project of 'universal common sense'.[20] Here, the critical faculty of judgement is constitutive of universal subjects, whose universality is guaranteed by the equal access to disinterested non-cognitive experience, available through nature and, secondarily, art. This is the *sensus communis* and sensibility from which Black (social) life is *a priori* and practically excluded, since Blackness and a subjectivity present to itself, or to others, do not coincide in Western modernity, insofar as this subjectivity constitutes the ground of both humanity and citizenship. This presents another dimension of the fraught relations between exceptionality and norm existing at the origins and throughout the life of artistic autonomy: every separation presupposes a more foundational and unthought exclusion, here from the very category of the human subject and its putatively universal modes of feeling. The violence of the norm is cancelled in the modality of the aesthetic, only to return at another level – the exclusion from rational humanity capable of suspending its self-mastery in the common enjoyment of aesthetic experience.

Therefore, against Kant's positive enlightenment project that enshrines art in the production of (white) universality as an agency

20 'Black' does not straightforwardly function as an identity category here (nor in the different projects around 'Blackness' undertaken by Fred Moten) – that is to say, it does not function *affirmatively*. Here, 'Black' is meant to denote not a phenotype but an ontological position with a complex relation to history and geopolitics; the main category that the experience of Blackness is read through is enslavement and its lasting necropolitical consequences. See also the important formulation in Saidiya Hartman, *Scenes of Subjection: Terror, Slavery, and Self-Making in Nineteenth-Century America*, rev. ed., New York: W. W. Norton, 2022: 'blackness is defined here in terms of social relationality rather than identity . . . it is a contested figure at the very center of social struggle' (94).

of common world-building, and, in fact, all concepts of critique that treat subjecthood as a form of property, Wilderson opposes a negative 'irreconcilable' project that wants to 'destroy the world'.[21] This brings us back to his invocation of the shortcomings of any politics of refusal that is limited to the frame of the existent and its premises: self-abolition is fated to failure unless it also attacks the presuppositions of its possibility, patriarchy, the (white) Human. I would argue that a subtle but thoroughgoing negativity of a similar type can be seen in Rowland's already mentioned *9102000*, in which objects that were produced in local prisons are presented as post-Duchampian readymades. These prisons are sites in which a racialised population does not 'own' its labour and cannot freely sell it, unlike the exceptional 'non-labour' of the artist.[22] The objects are rented by Rowland and are for rent in turn, eschewing both the status of a work and these objects' imbrication in an art market. There is a concern with making visible while avoiding the closures of representation, an approach that partakes of pre-modern allegory as much as of the conceptual décor or environment-as-ideology familiar from, for instance, the work of Marcel Broodthaers. We can likewise come back to 2016's *Disgorgement*, whose title is a legal term for reparations payable by insurance companies that still hold slave insurance policies on their books, taken out prior to the termination of

21 Frank B. Wilderson III, '"We're trying to destroy the world": Anti-blackness and police violence after Ferguson: An interview with Frank B. Wilderson III', *ill will editions*, 25 November 2014, ill-will-editions.tumblr.com.

22 Not all US prison labour is compulsory, but this does constitute one of the most highly restricted and disciplinary and therefore 'non-free' labour markets. See Whitney Benns, 'American slavery, reinvented', *The Atlantic*, 21 September 2015, theatlantic.com. See also Michelle Alexander, *The New Jim Crow: Mass Incarceration in the Age of Color-Blindness*, New York 2012; Gilmore, *Golden Gulag*.

that legal institution in the United States. For *Disgorgement*, Rowland has started a Reparations Purpose Trust, which holds shares in one of the named insurance companies, until such time as they are obligated to make the reparations payments through the passage of federal legislation in the US – legislation that has been introduced as a bill in Congress every year since 1989 without success. This really would be a payout contingent on 'the end of the world', in a limited manner of speaking.

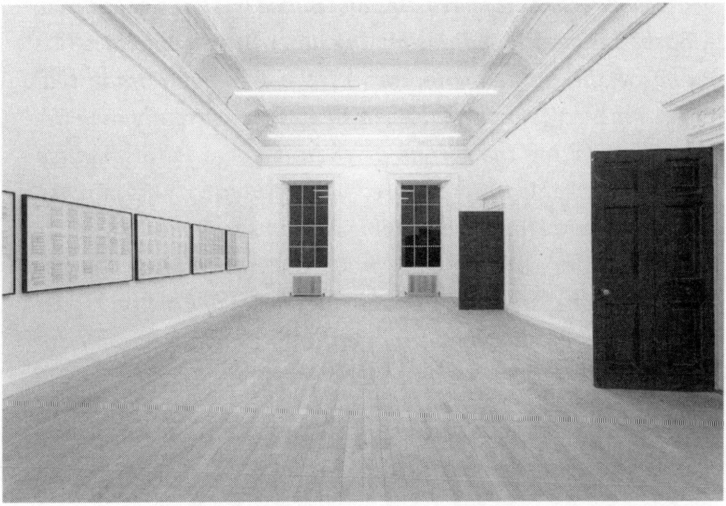

Cameron Rowland, *3 & 4 Will. IV c. 73*,
ICA, London, 2020, installation view

Artwork text: *The property relation of the enslaved included and exceeded that of chattel and real estate. Plantation mortgages exemplify the ways in which the value of people who were enslaved, the land they were forced to labor on, and the houses they were forced to maintain were mutually constitutive. Richard Pares writes that "[mortgages] became commoner and commoner until, by 1800, almost every large plantation debt was a mortgage debt." Slaves simultaneously functioned as collateral for the debts of their masters, while laboring intergenerationally under the debt of the master. The taxation of plantation products imported to Britain, as well as the taxation of interest paid to plantation lenders, provided revenue for Parliament and income for the monarch.*

Mahogany became a valuable British import in the 18th century. It was used for a wide variety of architectural applications and furniture, characterising Georgian and Regency styles. The timbers were felled and milled by slaves in Jamaica, Barbados, and Honduras among other British colonies. It is one of the few commodities of the triangular trade that continues to generate value for those who currently own it.

After taking the throne in 1820, George IV dismantled his residence, Carlton House, and the house of his parents, Buckingham House, combining elements from each to create Buckingham Palace. He built Carlton House Terrace between 1827 and 1832 on the former site of Carlton House as a series of elite rental properties to generate revenue for the Crown. All addresses at Carlton House Terrace are still owned by the Crown Estate, manager of land owned by the Crown since 1760.

12 Carlton House Terrace is leased to the Institute of Contemporary Arts. The building includes four mahogany doors and one mahogany handrail. These five mahogany elements were mortgaged by the Institute of Contemporary Arts to Encumbrance Inc. on January 16th, 2020 for £1000 each. These loans will not be repaid by the ICA. As security for these outstanding debts, Encumbrance Inc. will retain a security interest in these mahogany elements. This interest will constitute an encumbrance on the future transaction of 12 Carlton House Terrace. An encumbrance is a right or interest in real property that does not prohibit its exchange but diminishes its value. The encumbrance will remain on 12 Carlton House Terrace as long as the mahogany elements are part of the building. As reparation, this encumbrance seeks to limit the property's continued accumulation of value for the Crown Estate. The Crown Estate provides 75% of its revenue to the Treasury and 25% directly to the monarch.

Here too we see the mediation of the affirmative and negative – the way in which the tactic of blockage, as a transformation of the relationship between people, state and the materiality as well as abstraction of economic power, relates to abolition as a productive as well as 'destituting' tactic. In this sense, perhaps, the spirit of abolition can be extracted from property, *but not through the 'decision' of the enfranchised autonomous subject.* Rather, it can be achieved only by the tenets of the kind of graduated and tortuous legal realism that terms such as 'disgorgement' (the court-ordered return of ill-gotten gains) and 'encumbrance' (a type of lien) evoke – legal mechanisms that add friction to how a piece of the fictitious commodity of land is able to circulate, as in Rowland's *Depreciation* (2018), or that buy up shares in companies holding slave insurance policies intact from the era of the 'peculiar institution', pending reparations (*Disgorgement*, 2016). At *3 & 4 Will IV c. 73* at the ICA in London, Rowland punctures the value-retaining capacities of slave-industry-made goods now serving as Crown assets, leaving them still marketable, but less so than before (*Encumbrance*, 2020). As these assets include material infrastructure – the mahogany doors and banister of the ICA's Regency-period building, which still belong to the British monarchy (see photo above) – here the legal instrument of encumbrance becomes most akin to a species of termite. Commodity fetishism is riddled by termite tracks. The inescapable ownership relation between the ICA and the Crown Estate gets aerated by a parasitical one, which it has itself invited, sanctioned and signed. The deployment of the exhibiting institution as contractual partner in speculative ventures is one of the two main ways that property performs as a medium in Rowland's work. The other one is the reflexive location of property in the ownership relations of the artworks themselves, which are objects that are generally acquired rather than fabricated by Rowland or by any other purposefully artistic means. As we have already noted, if they are made available, it is under conditions of outright purchase, rental or rental at cost. These can at the same time be the conditions under which these objects enter the exhibition space, as with *Pacotille* (2020) and *Society* (2020) in the ICA show, or *Group of 8 Used Bikes – Item: 1284-018213* (2018) at MOCA LA, which was bought as a lot at a police auction as one of several groups of objects in the exhibition obtained through processes of civil asset forfeiture, a habitual money-spinner for cash-strapped police departments in the US, along with equally normalised if exponentially more grotesque practices such as billable probation (*Probation Order Under 18 U.S.C. § 3607*, 2020) or 'pay-to-stay' incarceration. This reflexivity about the conditions of the artist's participation in culture as a market agent, an instigator and delegator of various types of canny, brand-building action, and the resistance to separating this embedding from the histories and actualities staged by the work, is recursive. In its many-sided thoroughness, Rowland's approach puts you in mind of a crystal drill, if there is such an appliance. It creates sightlines by means of cutting through (language, provenances, histories) but the cutting apparatus is already a prism. The legal term 'discovery' seems apposite here, as if establishing a contractual relation creates some other vantage on its fixity.

This is a practice where legal realism bears great imaginative agency. A typical example is the ambiguous status of the enslaved person, which was real and nightmarish rather than metaphorical, but still provides one of the best optics for Rowland's parallaxes. As they write in the text for the show, 'The property relation of the enslaved included and exceeded that of chattel and real estate'.[23] As Ian Baucom also notes, in his discussion of enslaved people as both commodities and money capital, the 'double consciousness' of Blackness inside white supremacy identified by W. E. B. Du Bois had a parallel in the double consciousness of capital in the ways that enslaved subjects could be made to yield profit.[24]

The discursive complexity of this exhibition, as in all of Rowland's projects, feels both generous and like a vortex, finely imbricated with an affective undertow that somehow links the high-conceptual wall installation of the legal contract and the artefacts of disciplinary terror mounted a short distance away. Cattle brands used to burn a mark of ownership on the 'people' of a Barbadian evangelical mission in the eighteenth century hang on one wall, opposite an electronic monitor used today. The pieces create an echo of racialised terror administered via the flesh, which resonates painfully around the elegant room. Both objects recall an earlier work, the 2015 *HandPunch* photographic series, which pictured a biometric timeclock in various workplaces. This Postonian gadget, evoking the author of *Time, Labor and Social Domination*, acts as a memento of Rowland's ongoing focus on how abstraction is measured, managed and embodied.[25] What makes this abstraction real, of course – as real as the 'car that runs you over' (Lukács) – is, precisely, property relations and the

23 Cameron Rowland, '3 & 4 Will. C. 73', reprinted in *Mousse*, 24 April 2020, moussemagazine.it.

24 Ian Baucom, *Specters of the Atlantic: Finance Capital, Slavery, and the Philosophy of History*, Durham: Duke University Press, 2005, 17–28.

25 Moishe Postone, *Time, Labor, and Social Domination: A Reinterpretation of Marx's Critical Theory*, Cambridge: Cambridge University Press, 1993.

violent means of their enforcement in capitalist social life, which have never existed in anything other than a racialised form, as Cedric Robinson posits throughout his work.[26]

What would it mean to find desire in such an infrastructure, to brush against its dismal asperities? Rowland approaches the materiality of social infrastructures such as prisons and the judiciary as a type of 'hold', in something like Sharpe's, Moten's or Simone White's terms, and also the title of one of Rowland's own works from 2017: an ensemble of shipboard fastenings ('twist-locks') and marine insurance certificates.[27] A 'hold' that is not so much a melancholy fastness, or a nourishing enclave of compromised sociality, as a fraught container of antagonisms both expressed in, and suppressed by, the letter *and* the instrument of the law, which can just as easily be a print-out as a police lamp, to go by the inventory of this show. This is a history that is always present if constitutively elusive, driven by a logic which, as Bhandar notes, 'irrevocably fuses property and race together' as modes of abstraction.[28] Modes of abstraction like equality before the law, the democracy of money, the natural intimacies of property. The artefacts in Rowland's projects communicate a painful tremor, as banal objects with distinct backstories in the slave trade. At other times, they testify to this history with an obdurate wit, like the canal boat mooring rented for the purpose of not being used (*Mooring*, 2020), due to its being adjacent to the

26 Georg Lukács, *Marx's Basic Ontological Principles*, translated by David Fernbach, London: Merlin, 1978, 40; Cedric Robinson, *Black Marxism: The Making of the Black Radical Tradition*, New York: Penguin, 2021.

27 Christina Sharpe, *In the Wake: Blackness and Being*, Durham: Duke University Press, 2016, Chapter 3; Moten and Harney, *The Undercommons*, Chapter 6.

28 Brenna Bhandar, 'Property, Law, and Race: Modes of Abstraction', *UC Irvine Law Review*, 4, 1 (2014): 205.

previous site of a warehouse belonging to the Rathbone company, a large player in the Liverpool node of the triangular trade.[29] The dysphoria of the object in relation to the historico-legal complex, its infrastructural asymmetry, is unfathomably huge. The allegorical and the baroque come to the fore, which the proliferation of contract panels alongside mementos of confinement in the grand upstairs rooms in the ICA show reinforces. The oscillation between the functional, the critical and the aesthetic familiar from conceptualism's penchant for contracts (Michael Asher, Seth Siegelaub) and other administrative tools (Adrian Piper), as well as the institutional-critical strategies that involved reorderings of space, inventory and fixtures (Asher, Fred Wilson, John Knight), are a few of the coordinates that could be cited here. The distinct character of Rowland's approach, certainly with regard to Asher or Knight, is that there is no modification to the fabric of exhibition spaces, which may be due to the fact that the spaces are not the addressee. Invoked instead are the property relations in which they are enmeshed, and the modifications to those relations they are in a position to support. The institution becomes another of the sourced objects on display, whose aporetic histories are relentlessly filtered and arrayed.

The objects appear as repositories of systemic dependencies. As Eric Golo Stone put it in a piece from 2018, Rowland presents items 'without alteration', which is to say, in a non-proprietary way.[30] Nothing is changed about them except the means of circulation. They thus come into the space as evidence, or transitional objects – both as themselves and as crystals of abstract systems, a

29 The Rathbone company was a timber supplier, cotton importer and financial services provider in that order – a rather resonant historical sequence.

30 Eric Golo Stones, 'Legal Implications: Cameron Rowland's Rental Contract', *October*, 164 (2018).

feature they share with all commodities. They are object, image and (extensive) caption at the same time, recalling Walter Benjamin's terms of universal captioning as the potential politics of an all-consuming image space. Archaeology comes into play here, as well as the 'evidence-based' practices of forensic architecture, though perhaps only on one point: the way that documentation produces rather than stabilises reality. Each of Rowland's projects has centred on an institutional site's capacity to perform in its given role as well as constitute a party to a new contract, a capacity lent to it by capital and state. *3 & 4 Will. IV c. 73* zones in on the historical peculiarities of the British state, made perceptible and even unavoidable in physical infrastructure leased from the monarchy, an institution that was sustained for centuries by the slave trade, then by the moral and economic capital of its abolition across and beyond its imperial possessions. Real estate and nationhood come packaged together here in a way they couldn't quite do in New York, LA, Cologne or Brussels. And what is it but real estate and nationalism that diminish the possibilities of earthly life, especially in London? The abstractions can't help but take a more congealed form in the building of the ICA, while devalorisation slowly fills the rooms you've just left 'like a spirit, a gas'.[31]

31 Gilles Deleuze, 'Postscript on the Societies of Control', *October*, 59 (Winter 1992), 4: 'In a society of control, the corporation has replaced the factory, and the corporation is a spirit, a gas.'

Conclusion

Critique Is the Cutting Tool, Not the Price of Admission

A lot of contemporary theory today mobilises concepts of totalisation, whether these are feel-good concepts such as multitude or feel-bad concepts such as negation, abolition and world destruction. The role of infrastructural critique, in an optimistic reading, is to put these concepts in motion from their pinnacle of traumatised radicalism, to make them speculative rather than totalising, whether through interventionist gestures such as Black's, theoretical contributions like Hartman's or Moten's, or artistic works like Rowland's. What I want to emphasise is that this is not a project of epistemic regulation and intellectual hygiene: it is a kind of unfreezing of the fast-fixed, one that can also happen within collective processes of debate, education, organising and struggle. Whereas holding abstractly radical positions often leads to disappointment and a withdrawal from all those things, and a basically, if not always theoretically, conservative standpoint at the end of the day – or a fidelity to radicalism, but relocated to the right, where history and mediation really don't matter as they're submerged into violent myth – other approaches to the totality retain their speculative negativity. Throughout this book, I have tried to point to the critical dimension of building stuff and abducting resources, stuff that allows you to materially weaken the enemy by practically and ideologically eroding their legitimacy because the means of – at least – social reproduction are at your disposal. So, really, we're always talking about practical critique, and many theories of abolition can be conceived entirely in the same spirit, because there's no opposition between breaking and building if you approach the parameters of reality speculatively.[1]

Cameron Rowland's practice has been central to the presentation here due to the way it mediates between the most abstract (legal-financial instruments) and the most concrete (embodied histories of slavery persisting into the present). Approaches like theirs are key to understanding and transforming the present, because the racism, direct domination, exploitation, extraction, financial abstraction and murder that have characterised capitalism as a global system from its inception have escalated in the present and are likely to continue. The conjugation of infrastructural critique (spanning legal, financial, artistic and organisational infrastructures) in Rowland's art provides a model for thinking about the relations between totalisation and blockage – between tactics and scale – as well as a materialist insight into what it is necessary to think for and against, in a time when biological life is directly threatened by the prospect of the form that life takes in our societies continuing unabated, un-negated.

As the art theorist Max Haiven recently wrote, the imbrication of artists and institutions with wider movements for the abolition of the wage, property, race and gender, at least on their far horizon, might also entail the abolition of the artist as an 'economic figure'.[2] The justification for this, and it is vital to articulate it in such terms, is that the creative subject is among the most brutalised of all capitalist subjects, since not only is competitive and mendacious behaviour inculcated as employability, but the

1 For a contemporary overview, published shortly after the George Floyd uprising, when this passage was written, see Ruth Wilson Gilmore, *Abolition Geography: Essays Towards Liberation*, London: Verso, 2022.

2 Max Haiven, 'No Artists Left Alive', *Arts of the Working Class*, 23 April 2024, artsoftheworkingclass.org.

subject's right to engage in such behaviour is justified in terms principally transcendent of the economy and survival motives: creativity, inspiration, magic. The creative industries should thus be considered just as much unfiltered playgrounds of capitalist theology as the financial industries, which at least host subjectivities convinced they are in it for reasons (usually venal) other than to further the fortunes of finance as a moving spirit of progress in the world. In the artworld today, in which the content is often as radical as the practice is conformist, the task, as I wrote earlier, is to actualise exceptionality, to make generative use of the negativity *that is already there*, disregarding institutional boundaries between inside and outside and treating infrastructure pragmatically as a way of enabling movements for a concrete something else. In the circumstances in which we find ourselves, anything that is not about construction, anything that is not practical, that does not mediate organisation/antagonism/struggle in the most wide-ranging and concrete sense is to be resisted. Anything that weaves ontological spells against the urgency of specific tasks of transformation is to be resisted. Abstract radicalism is everywhere and it is to be resisted. Affect drowning mediation and contradiction is to be resisted. Reproductive realism is of course to be resisted, even if this problem seems less prominent to me now than it did a few years ago, given how thoroughly it's been recuperated by managerial strata as a 'humane' justification for layoffs and attacks on working conditions.

Rather, as Rowland's work shows, the changes to be contemplated and enacted should be drawn from the generative negativity of history and experience, which can emerge in situations of antagonism (direct contestation of the complacency and cynicism of power), appropriation (the 'destituent' emptying out of the resources which capital extracts in order to do violence to us), and abolition (determinate negation not only of a harmful institution, or practice, but of all the ways of accommodating it that have become socially habitual).[3] In the present book these remain, of course, only fragmented and intuitive hints rather than propositions. However, their direction of travel is, as already noted, that of negation, but negation as a process that is constantly differentiating itself and creating other possibilities. How to draw the boundary between this restless negativity as a guiding rope for emancipation and the hopeless mutability of a society committing suicide-by-commodity remains an enormous array of questions for another day – a day that cannot be postponed.

Finally, all these tasks point to the need to understand the concept of critique at issue in 'infrastructural critique'. The perspective argued for here cannot leave critique in its own right untouched, with its acknowledged genealogy in the unconditional autonomy of the isolated and European-identified Enlightenment subject that rightly informs most debates around the notion in the sphere of radical theory these days. Instead, the aim is to contribute to the comparatively sidelined history of critique as a material practice of antagonism whose subject, if it has one, is dispersive, uncategorisable and collective. The resources necessary to flesh out this other practice of critique, in an apparent paradox, owe substantially to contemporary debates around 'identity politics', inasmuch as those debates can also show the salience of a relational non-identity and negativity for any notion of critique that would make claims on the infrastructure that provides it with its conditions – that is to say, with the material possibilities of critique as well as its object. When Hannah Black writes about 'the self as historical and social material' in the space of art, a self that entails a non-identity with the 'real structures of "identity"', she is describing identity as a structure imposed on the non-white, non-male cultural worker, whether it's by liberal arts institutions looking to burnish their inclusion agendas or 'identity critics' such as

3 Petrossiants, 'Preliminary Notes Towards a Destituent Art'.

the ones who phobically denounce trans people, or argue that 'identities' are distractions from class struggle.[4] In this negative and problematic concept of 'identity', which is itself identitarian insofar as it treats class as a 'flatly individual and experiential category', there is a contradiction between identity and non-identity that recalls Adorno's Hegelian appropriation of the latter, but also visibly Hegel's own argument in the *Science of Logic*, when he notes that 'Essence is mere Identity and reflection in itself only as it is self-relating negativity, and in that way self-repulsion. It contains therefore essentially the characteristic of Difference.'[5] Conversely, infrastructural critique is defined by the tension between clarifying negativity when it identifies its opponents and the difference that traverses its own speaking position. Critique then becomes the practice of non-identity, a self-relating negativity beyond essence. It is the irreconcilability without end of social antagonism in the institution of art and its real-world spaces, even as they programmatically commit to inclusion to undercut their own status as infrastructures of domination. This antagonism is turned into aporia, insoluble, and perhaps not even interesting, within the framework of the institution – that is, at the level of programming – but as soon as it gains a transversal dimension by looking to the infrastructure, there is a gain (one could even call it a 'gain of function') in the capacity of critique, to not only query its own conditions of existence, but to see how the resources of critique itself can provide infrastructure for other fights that pull the institution into their vortex.

4 Black, 'The Identity Artist and the Identity Critic'.

5 G. W. F. Hegel, *The Logic of Hegel, Translated from the Encyclopaedia of the Philosophical Sciences*, translated by William Wallace, Oxford: Oxford University Press, 1904, 215.

Acknowledgements

... it came to me that the basic condition of history is that it be collective. If it is personal, it is only lost time.

This book was always a collective project, even before we had to step in to finish it. We hope its existence goes some way towards acknowledging the debt we owe, collectively, to Marina, who never lost any time, and who always gave everything to us.

Our editorial work has been primarily focused on how to arrange the material. We know others would have made other decisions, not least Marina herself. We did our best under the circumstances. At the same time, we hope the provisionality of this volume expresses something true about Marina's approach at the level of its method: about a form of critique, that is, that is not 'tragically incomplete' but radically open, which is to say mutable and unfinishable, in a similar sense to other enduring works of critical analysis that remain porous to their changing historical present, and deeply connected with the practice, always shifting and experimental, of emancipatory struggle.

To those who helped us to track down, archive or assemble Marina's hundreds of texts, we owe a huge debt of gratitude: to Karolin Meunier, Romana Schmalisch, Antonia Majaca and Luciano Pecoits, but especially to Tomislav Medak and Marcel Mars at the Public Library / Memory of the World for their development of the Marina Vishmidt Collected Works, where all of the working materials used to construct this book will eventually be hosted, so that others can develop their own approach to its 'gaps, rather than voids'. We owe gratitude to Luisa Lorenza Corna, Hannah Proctor and Andreas Petrossiants for carefully reading and commenting on the manuscript. For support in Vienna with the conference 'What Is Infrastructural Critique?', we owe thanks to Rose-Anne Gush, Sofia Bempeza, Helmut Draxler, Antonia Birnbaum, Annette Krauss and Alexi Kukuljevic, as well as the conference participants, Marwa Arsanios, Mattin Artiach, Hannah Black, Maria Bussmann, Taylor Le Melle, Romana Schmalisch and Robert Schlicht, Kerstin Schroedinger and Angela Melitopoulos, Natascha Sadr Haghighian and Alberto Toscano, and the many conference assistants and attendees. For the 'Conditions of Possibility' of *Mute* magazine, to Anthony Iles, Pauline van Mourik Broekman, Dimitra Kotouza, Josephine Berry, Mira Mattar, Benedict Seymour. For the collective reading of Marina's 'Known Nowheres' at Historical Materialism 2024, to Hannah Black, Christina Chalmers, Dimitra Kotouza, Rose-Anne Gush, FTC Manning, Zoe Sutherland. For the other panels at HM, to Anthony Iles, Avigail Moss, Roberto Mozzachiodi, Paul Rekret, Jack Segbars, Daniel Spaulding, Stewart Martin, Steve Edwards, Sebastian Budgen. For the Marina's Cues colloquium at Leuphana University, we owe gratitude to Susanne Leeb and Thomas Krutak, as well as Maria Chehonadskih, Alexei Penzin, Blaise Kirschner, Lizzie Homersham, Sam Dolbear, and the other contributors mentioned elsewhere in these acknowledgements, and for the *Radical Philosophy* dossier on Marina's work to Ray Brassier, E. C. Feiss, Daniel Spaulding and Zoe Sutherland. For the time spent discussing Marina's work at the Performing Arts Forum in spring 2025, to many people, but especially Stefa Govaart, Steph Holl-Trieu, Andrea Rodrigo and Nikhil Vettukattil. For their preface and for their example, to Stefano Harney and Fred Moten. Thank you.

Marina's friends and central collaborators are present everywhere in her work: Em Hedditch, Melanie Gilligan, Melissa Gordon, Chris Evans, Anthony Iles, Zoe Sutherland, Karolin Meunier, Andreas Petrossiants, Ruth Buchanan, Grace Schwindt, Jakob Jakobsen, the members of Cinenova, the members of the Feminist Reading Group, the members of Channels, the members of Full Unemployment Cinema, the members of Goldsmiths UCU, the members of the Feminist Art Maintenance Group. In the absence of material drawn from Andreas's conversation with Marina, first published on the blog of Historical Materialism in 2020, this book would have been greatly impoverished.

Ash Reid and Thomas Watson shared important recordings of interviews with Marina in which she spoke about her life and work; Maralea Lutino and Ellie Farrell shared memories of jumping turnstiles in NYC; the team at Pelican House in Bethnal Green shared space. Many others shared skills and resources in order to make Marina's memorial – an important learning space for all of us – possible. A number of artists who informed Marina's thinking about infrastructural critique provided access to their work, or helped us to track down what Marina wrote about it: Dora Budor, Cameron Rowland, Ghislaine Leung, Carolyn Lazard, Ima-Abasi Okon, Nicholas Mangan, Joshua Schwebel. The Leuphana Institute for Advanced Studies in Culture and Society made Kerstin and Danny welcome in Lüneburg in Marina's absence. Lizzie Homersham, Nikolaus Perneczcy, the Perneczcy family, Sam Dolbear, Ciarán Finlayson, Dave Beech, Shela Sheikh, James Burton, Onyeka Igwe, Justin Katko, David Grundy, Luke Roberts, Amy Tobin, Amy De'Ath, Sabeth Buchmann, Carol Hayward, Andy Hayward, William Rowe, M. Caye Castagnetto, Sam Dolbear, Olia Sosnovskaya, Aleksei Borisionok, Blaise Kirschner, Anja Büchele, Matthew Hyland, Rachel Baker, Tanya Singh, Noah Brehmer, Darsavini, John Cunningham, Anne Boyer, Jacob-Bard Rosenberg, Mike Sperlinger, Gail Day, David

Panos, Emily Pethick, Sven Lütticken, Rob Lucas, Nina Steiert, Andy Steiert, Angela Dimitrakaki, Fulvia Carnevale, Maria Iorio and Raphaël Cuomo, as well as too many others to mention, all supported this project in various ways. Thank you.

The editors and curators of *Mousse*, Halle für Kunst Steiermark, *Camera Austria* and the *Journal of Science and Technology of the Arts* kindly gave permission to reprint articles reworked in Chapters 1, 2, 3 and 6. Mierle Laderman Ukeles very generously allowed us to use an image from her *Touch Sanitation Performance* on the cover.

Finally, our love and gratitude to Nina and Carmelo Mendez.

Index

abjection, 8, 21, 52, 114, 118, 122, 160
abolition, 4, 22–6, 28, 109, 155–7, 159, 163–81
'absolute commodity', 87
accumulation, 51, 101, 106, 109, 118, 139, 143, 154, 158–9, 173
Adorno, Theodor W., 3, 42, 46–7, 87, 101–2, 113, 151–2, 160
  Aesthetic Theory, 87, 113
  Negative Dialectics, 42, 151–2
aesthetics, 30, 40–1, 52, 56, 60, 141, 157
afro-pessimism, 161
Akerman, Chantal, 137
alterity, 44, 89
Althusser, Louis, 117
antagonism, ix, 31, 37, 43, 48, 55, 63, 156, 159, 176, 181–3
anti-Blackness, 43, 96, 170
apotropaic vaudeville, 66
Arendt, Hannah, 45
Arthur, Christopher J., 164
art institutions, 23–5, 27, 55–6, 59–61, 65–9, 71–2, 74–5, 87–8, 91–2, 103–4, 106–9, 118, 120–1, 131, 158
artistic labour, 39–40, 102, 104–5, 126
  politics of, 106
Art Workers' Coalition, 66–8
Asher, Michael, 11, 67, 177
autoimmunity, 128, 130
automatic subject, 87
autonomy, ix, 14, 44, 46, 49, 65, 105, 126, 130, 160
  artistic, 44–5, 70, 160, 169
autonomist Marxism, 89, 101, 106
Azoulay, Ariella, 168

Bateson, Gregory, 128
Beech, Dave, 159, 187
Benjamin, Walter, 29, 77, 80, 85
Black, Hannah, 41, 162, 165–6, 182, 186
Black Marxism, 176
Black studies, ix, 26, 45, 156, 167
Boltanski, Luc, 69
Brenna, Bhandar, 152, 168, 176
Broodthaers, Marcel, 170
Buchloh, Benjamin, 20, 77
Budor, Dora, 97–8, 101, 187
Butler, Judith, 30

care, 9, 13, 15, 53–4, 116
Channels, 8, 10, 29
chattel slavery, 57, 155–6
Chen, Chris, 139

Chiapello, Eve, 69
Chto Delat, 19
circulation, 55, 105, 134, 157, 177
citizenship, 40, 169
Claire Fontaine, 121, 165
class struggle, 102, 106, 151, 183
Clover, Joshua, 55
Combahee River Collective, 43
communisation, 3–4, 21, 23
complicity, 24, 85, 91
conditions, 25–6, 30–1, 37, 39–40, 44–5, 49–50, 52–3, 69–70, 84–5, 91–2, 103–6, 113–15, 117–19, 125–32, 137–8, 146–7, 156, 163–4, 174, 181–3
  materialist theory of, 26–7, 32
Conrad, Tony, 126
contemporary art, 23–4, 26, 42, 49, 70, 74, 94, 98, 102, 154, 160–1, 172
contracts, 15, 104, 107, 116, 166, 177
  civil, 167–8
contradictions, 8–9, 65, 69–70, 85, 87, 131–2, 152–4, 156, 159–60, 181, 183
counter-reification device, 15
Covid-19 pandemic, 54
creativity, 42, 45–6, 62, 78, 80, 118, 181
Creischer, Alice, 73
Crimean Bridge, 58
crisis, 18, 20, 51, 90, 116, 140, 159, 164
critique, 14–15, 17, 23, 25, 27–9, 49–51, 54–5, 63, 65–87, 89–90, 92, 100, 102, 179, 181–3
  infrastructures of, 29, 41, 79
  institution of, 65, 73–4, 76
critical infrastructure, 50
cryptocurrencies, 147
cultural workers, 78, 91, 105–6, 151
culture industry, 39, 160
curators, 23, 71, 75, 126, 188
cuts, 2, 24, 92–5, 97, 100, 151, 174, 179

De'Ath, Amy, 166
Debord, Guy, 5
debts, 140, 172, 185
Decolonize This Place, 55, 85, 91, 162
defunctionalisation, 121
Deleuze, Gilles, 3, 9, 12, 18, 26, 93, 155, 178
dematerialisation, 144
dependencies, 47, 78, 103, 119, 123, 125–6, 132–5, 177
Derrida, Jacques, 97
desedimentation, 154
destitution, 157, 173 182
Detroit techno, 38
dialectic, 44, 46, 117, 119, 138, 152, 161
  speculative, 152
difference, 7–8, 10, 25–6, 34, 42–3, 93–4, 100, 104, 151, 153, 183
Dillemuth, Stephan, 70
Dimitrakaki, Angela, 13
disability, 126–30, 135
  social model of, 127, 130

disavowal, 52, 104
dispossession, 40, 46, 56, 168
  accumulation by, 139
Diversity of Aesthetics, 41, 157
DIY cultures, 31, 32, 39, 61, 71
documentary, 49, 84, 147
domination, 53, 100, 149, 165, 175, 183
'double bind', 65, 128, 130, 156
double freedom, 69, 78
Duchamp, Marcel, 123, 133, 138
ducks, 15, 23
dumbwaiters, 92–4
dysfunction, 157

ecology, 22, 43–4, 59, 81, 91, 104, 129, 139–42, 150, 153
economy, 12, 47, 67, 85, 149, 158, 181
  circular, 98, 148–9, 153
  libidinal, 66
education, 40, 127, 158, 179
emancipation, 87, 182
enclosures, x, 99
Endnotes (journal), 3, 4, 21, 23, 96, 118, 140, 166
endo-colonisation, 158
energy, 138, 142–3, 147
energy infrastructure, 149
Engelhard, Anna, 58
Enlightenment, 65, 169, 182
entanglement, 53, 75, 94
entrepreneurship, 42, 46, 70
entropy, 30, 120, 137–54, 160
ethics, 53, 127, 139, 141
exceptionality, 39–40, 78, 101, 139, 158–9, 169
exchange, 48, 100, 134, 139, 172
exchange-value, 14
exhaustion, 69, 134–5, 139–40
experimental totalisations, 45
experimentation, 45, 47, 62, 121
exploitation, 21, 38, 41, 80, 105, 107–8, 128, 139, 157, 165, 180
  racialised, 108
extraction, 40, 51, 53, 138–40, 142–4, 148, 158, 180

Federici, Silvia, 122, 159
feminism, 12, 22, 26, 31, 54, 73, 114, 116, 118, 124, 165
Ferreira da Silva, Denise, 47–8, 52–3, 74, 168
fetishism, 158–9, 167
fibreoptic cables, 54
finance, ix, 29, 42, 45–7, 53, 81, 156, 181
  speculative, 44
financialisation, 40, 55
Finlayson, Ciarán, 162
Firestone, Shulamith, 5
Floyd, George, 107, 180
Floyd, Kevin, 108, 139
Flusser, Vilém, 50
Forum Theatre, 83, 86
Foucault, Michel, 51
fracking, 143
frame, 11–12, 17, 49, 53, 75, 113–15, 118, 162, 170
Fraser, Andrea, 11, 20, 23, 66–7, 73–4, 77, 87, 145
Frazer, LaToya Ruby, 120
freedom, 42, 45, 47, 52, 70, 79, 145, 157, 165–6
Fried, Michael, 126

Fulci, Lucio, 25
funfair egalitarianism, 19
fungibility, 122

gaps, 2, 9, 55, 95–100, 108, 186
Gaza, 162
gender, 21, 25, 37–8, 79, 85, 108, 118–19, 124, 135, 137, 141
  logic of, 166
gentrification, 3, 46, 140
gesturality, 49, 77, 106, 108
Gibson, Jasmine, 135
Gilmore, Ruth Wilson, 51, 141, 170
Gonzalez, Maya, 21
Guattari, Félix, 155
Guerrilla Girls, 66

Harney, Stefano, 45, 80, 176
Harrison, Matthew Angelo, 101
Hartman, Saidiya, 156–7, 167–9, 179
Haslett, Tobi, 162
Hegel, G. W. F., 27, 47–8, 54, 152, 160, 168, 183
Heizer, Michael, 144
housework, 10, 121–3, 137, 154
human strike, 121, 165
Husni-Bey, Adelita, 60

identity, 41, 43, 100, 114, 119, 152, 169, 182–3
  antagonistic, 151
  speculative, 12, 16, 31, 42, 163
identity politics, 182
identity thinking, 42, 151
ideological state apparatuses, 117
immanence, 22, 25–6, 40, 67–8
indexicality, 29, 97, 134
individual, vii, 102, 105, 117, 127–8, 131, 132, 156, 159, 183
indigenous communities, 130, 144
industrial civilisation, 145–6, 153
Institute of Contemporary Art (ICA), 156, 172–4, 177–8
institutional critique, 20, 22, 24, 31, 33, 56–7, 62, 65–6, 68, 70–3, 77, 109, 113

Jackson, George, ix
Jorn, Asger, 15
justice, 102–3, 131, 139, 165

Kafka, Franz, 66
Kanders, Warren, 103, 162
Kant, Immanuel, 70, 147, 168–9
Kantianism, x, 27, 62, 65, 74, 92, 113, 138, 169
Kerch Strait, 59
Klossowski, Pierre, 16
Kluge, Alexander, x, 76
Kotouza, Dimitra, 186

labour, ix, 40, 42, 45–9, 51, 73, 76, 78–81, 86–7, 102–6, 115–20, 126–8, 138, 148, 166–7
  abstract, viii, 46
  gendered, 122, 132, 137
  immaterial, 78
  in art, 49, 102, 104, 106
labour-power, 77, 79, 115, 140, 168
Land Art, 143–4, 147, 153

law, 58, 85, 152, 170–1, 173–7, 180
Lazard, Carolyn, 28, 124, 125–8, 130–2, 135
LD50, 20
Le Guin, Ursula K., 96
Lenin, Vladimir, 117
Leung, Ghislaine, 125, 132–3, 135
Levi-Strauss, Claude, 146
Lippard, Lucy, 68
Lloyd, David, 52, 168
love, ix, xi–xii, 9, 12, 32, 140
Lukács, Gyorg, 175, 176
Luxemburg, Rosa, xii, 139, 158

McArthur, Park, 120
Macherey, Pierre, 165–6
Martens, Renzo, 161
Martin, Reinhold, 94
Marx, Karl, vii, 3, 5, 46, 69, 87, 115, 139–40, 151–2, 159
  Capital, Vol. I, 87, 140
Marxist-feminism, 10, 14, 21, 80, 115
materialism, 30, 125, 139, 141
  'burdened', 156
materials, 6–7, 11, 45, 48–9, 67, 69, 94, 97, 113, 149, 151, 185, 187
Mattin, 22, 87
Mbembe, Achille, 96
mediations, 9, 13, 17–18, 26, 31, 157–8, 163, 173, 179
medical-industrial complex, 130
metamorphosis, 12, 95
method, 5, 11–12, 25, 29, 32, 37, 48, 63, 118, 153, 185
Mezzadra, Sandro, 53, 81, 135
Mies, Maria, 159
mimesis, 70, 161
Mitchell, Timothy, 58, 138, 149
Mitropoulos, Angela, 165–6
modernity, 71, 81, 157, 168
money, 14, 46, 82, 91–2, 176
Moore, Jason W., 139–40
Morris, Robert, 56
Moten, Fred, x, 26, 44–5, 80, 165–6, 168–9, 176, 179

nature, 51, 91, 116, 137–9, 147, 169
  cheap, 139–40
  'second', 53–4
necropolitics, 96, 169
negation, 2, 18, 102, 105, 122–3, 156, 162–3, 165, 167–8, 179, 182
  determinate, 154, 160, 181
  institutions of, 74, 94
negation-as-autonomy, 161
negation-as-struggle, 161
negativity, 6–7, 12, 25–6, 32, 34, 89, 96–7, 117, 119, 164, 166, 181–3
  activated, 159
  generative, 181
Negt, Oskar, x, 76–7
Neilson, Brett, 53, 81, 135
NFTs (non-fungible tokens), 47, 142–3, 147–8, 153
NGOs, 161
Nicula, Elisabeth, 142, 144, 147–8
non-identity, 8, 42–3, 47, 99–100, 151–3, 182–3
  relational, 182

non-productive attitude, 70
norms, 9–10, 84, 151, 153, 168–9

ontology, 134, 154, 168
Oppenheim, Méret, 101
Ottinger, Ulrike, 5
organising, 38–9, 44, 62, 87, 91, 102, 104, 107–8, 149, 151, 179
Osborne, Peter, 134–5, 156
Osten, Marion von, 71, 73, 75, 78, 81, 87

pacification, 86
Palestine, 50, 55,
pandemic, 27, 50, 55, 108
paradox of self-abolition, 22
Parente, Letícia, 16, 122
Pateman, Carole, 165–6
pathos-structure, 78, 100
patriarchy, 66, 159, 170
pedagogy, 52, 71, 105, 158
performativity, 58, 87, 98, 133, 162
personality, 8–9, 16, 100
Petrossiants, Andreas, 28, 32, 41, 157, 182
Piper, Adrian, 177
police violence, 52, 55, 84, 162, 170
political economy, 16–17, 27, 77, 87, 108, 140
PopeL., William, 66
Postone, Moishe, 175
precarity, 3, 69, 76, 78–9, 104–5, 107
prisms, 62, 79, 174
prisons, 51, 56, 170, 176
property relations, viii, 171, 175, 177

rabbit-ducks, 30, 32
race, ix, 4, 37, 39, 51–2, 56, 106, 108, 118, 176, 180
  metaphysics of, 74
racialisation, 52, 140–1, 167
Ramsden, Mel, 77
Raspé, Margaret, 13, 20, 30
Raunig, Gerald, 73
realism, 30
  empirical, 156
  legal, 173–4
recursivity, 11–13, 24, 29, 31
reflexivity, 56, 61, 78, 84, 174
refusal, 14, 41, 80–1, 105, 119, 135, 153, 164, 170
repetition, 25–6, 34, 93–4
representation, 2, 11, 30, 44, 52, 123, 131–2, 141, 148, 168, 170
reproduction, 14, 18, 20–2, 24–5, 27–8, 52, 54–5, 89, 113–35, 138, 140, 158–9, 164–6
  conditions of, 41, 51–2, 114, 117
  institutional, 154
  of capital, 21, 116–17, 140
  of life, 115, 117–18
reproductive labour, 11, 13, 24, 78, 106, 114, 118–21, 135, 137, 140
'reproductive realism', 11, 13, 15, 19–20, 30, 89–90, 95, 108, 181
resources, 50–1, 53–4, 61–2, 69, 108, 114, 139, 143–4, 147, 181–3, 187
riot, xi, 55

riot grrrl, 37
Robinson, Cedric, ix, 176
Rouch, Jean, 66
Rowland, Cameron, viii, 5, 28, 57, 78, 120, 155, 156, 170–1, 174–7, 179, 180–1

sabotage, 21, 54–5
self-abolition, 3–4, 22, 137, 164–7, 170
self-valorisation, 117
Sharpe, Christina, 157, 176
Sherman, Zandi, 51
Siegelaub, Seth, 177
Siekmann, Andreas, 73
slave insurance policies, 56, 170, 173
slavery, 93, 167, 169, 175
  persistence of, 180
slaves, 16, 160, 172
Smithson, Robert, 145–6
social movements, 4, 55, 94, 102, 122, 130, 162
social reproduction, 12, 89–90, 114–17, 123, 127–8, 141, 143, 179
solidarity, 41, 55, 92, 162
speculation, 2–3, 7, 12, 14, 25, 27, 31–2, 34, 39, 42–3, 45–8, 60, 62
speculative negativity, viii, 179
Stakemeier, Kerstin, 14, 107, 129
Strau, Josef, 70
Strike MoMA, 55
stuckness, 8
subcultures, 71, 72
subject-formation, ix, 20
subjectivity, 33–4, 42, 54, 79–81, 119, 121, 169
sublimity, 147–8
supplement, logic of the, 97
surrealism, 99, 101, 108
survival, 14, 50, 89, 127, 129, 131
Sutherland, Zoe, 108, 123, 141
Syria, 50

Takala, Pilvi, 28, 75, 83–4, 86–7
temporality, 45, 59, 92, 135, 146
terror, 100, 137, 169, 175
totalisation, 23, 179–80
  false, 24, 28, 95
totality, 7, 44, 108, 139, 155, 168, 179
transversality, 41, 68–9, 70, 81, 87, 102, 106, 153
Trecartin, Ryan, 76

Ukeles, Mierle Laderman, x, 16, 121–33, 133, 154
Ukraine, 50
The Undercommons, 45, 80, 176
unionisation, 107, 148, 151
universals, concrete, 101, 107
unthought, position of the, 167–8
use-value, 14, 87, 160
usefulness, 14, 49, 120, 131, 137
uselessness, 119, 123

VALIE EXPORT, 66
valorisation, 43, 49, 53, 75, 87, 122, 158
value subjectivity, 19
violence, 60, 82, 101, 106, 120, 140, 166, 168–9, 181
  law-preserving, 85
  structural, 67, 91, 108

Vishmidt, Marina
Reproducing Autonomy, 14, 129
Speculation as a Mode of Production, 2, 3, 7, 12, 14, 25, 27, 42, 46, 70, 105, 121, 139, 152, 164
voids, 95, 101, 142, 144, 186
production of, 143, 147–8
socio-historical, 101
vulnerability, viii, 30, 91, 119, 132
group-differentiated, 51

war, 50, 59, 108, 144, 162
waste, 8–9, 12, 16, 119, 123, 140–3, 145, 148–9, 154, 160
entropic, 139, 142
White, Simone, 155
Wikstrom, Lindsey, 149–50
Wilderson III, Frank B., 96–7, 168, 170
Wilson, Fred, 177
white supremacy, 66, 68, 115–16, 130, 175
work, vii, 28, 37–9, 48, 56, 80, 82–4, 103–5, 113–14, 119, 121, 123–4, 126–7, 132, 145–7, 150–1, 153–7, 170, 174–6, 186–7
worker-as-entrepreneur, vii
Wynter, Sylvia, 52

Yemen, 50